CAMBRIDGE
UNIVERSITY PRESS

CAMBRIDGE PRIMARY
Global Perspectives

Learner's Skills Book 2

Adrian Ravenscroft

CAMBRIDGE
UNIVERSITY PRESS

Shaftesbury Road, Cambridge CB2 8BS, United Kingdom

One Liberty Plaza, 20th Floor, New York, NY 10006, USA

477 Williamstown Road, Port Melbourne, VIC 3207, Australia

314–321, 3rd Floor, Plot 3, Splendor Forum, Jasola District Centre, New Delhi – 110025, India

103 Penang Road, #05–06/07, Visioncrest Commercial, Singapore 238467

Cambridge University Press is part of the University of Cambridge.

It furthers the University's mission by disseminating knowledge in the pursuit of education, learning and research at the highest international levels of excellence.

www.cambridge.org
Information on this title: www.cambridge.org/9781009354172

First published 2024

20 19 18 17 16 15 14 13 12 11 10 9 8 7 6 5

Printed in Malaysia by Vivar Printing.

A catalogue record for this publication is available from the British Library

ISBN 978-1-009-35417-2 Learner's Skills Book 2 Paperback with Digital Access (1 Year)
ISBN 978-1-009-35806-4 Learner Skills Book 2 – eBook

Endorsement statement

Endorsement indicates that a resource has passed Cambridge International's rigorous quality-assurance process and is suitable to support the delivery of a Cambridge International curriculum framework. However, endorsed resources are not the only suitable materials available to support teaching and learning, and are not essential to be used to achieve the qualification. Resource lists found on the Cambridge International website will include this resource and other endorsed resources.

Any example answers to questions taken from past question papers, practice questions, accompanying marks and mark schemes included in this resource have been written by the authors and are for guidance only. They do not replicate examination papers. In examinations the way marks are awarded may be different. Any references to assessment and/or assessment preparation are the publisher's interpretation of the curriculum framework requirements. Examiners will not use endorsed resources as a source of material for any assessment set by Cambridge International.

While the publishers have made every attempt to ensure that advice on the qualification and its assessment is accurate, the official curriculum framework, specimen assessment materials and any associated assessment guidance materials produced by the awarding body are the only authoritative source of information and should always be referred to for definitive guidance. Cambridge International recommends that teachers consider using a range of teaching and learning resources based on their own professional judgement of their learners' needs.

Cambridge International has not paid for the production of this resource, nor does Cambridge International receive any royalties from its sale. For more information about the endorsement process, please visit www.cambridgeinternational.org/endorsed-resources

Contents

Introduction

Welcome to Stage 2 of **Cambridge Primary Global Perspectives.**
We hope you will find the projects in this book interesting.

You are going to work on four projects. The projects in this book help you understand new things.

The projects are about:

- the food we eat
- things we throw away
- practical activities we do
- moving to new places.

You will have learning goals.

The learning goals help you know what to do.

There are four children in the book.

They try out all of the projects.

Here is Zara.

Here is Marcus.

Here is Arun.

Here is Sofia.

You do not need to learn facts. You will need to help people.

You will learn how to:

- find out new facts
- find out what people think
- talk to lots of people
- think about what you do.

You will need to work in different ways.

- sometimes you will work on your own
- sometimes you will work with a partner or in a group
- sometimes you will learn in the classroom
- sometimes you will learn in different places.

There are lots of ways to do well:

- think about your own ideas
- think about other people's ideas
- help other learners to learn
- try out new ways to learn
- help other people to learn new things.

I hope you will enjoy the projects in this book!

Adrian Ravenscroft

How to use this book

In this book you will find lots of different things to help your learning.

Activities at the start of a project to help you understand what you will be doing.

Getting started
1 With your class, look at the pictures and talk about the questions.   • What are the people doing?   • What are the children finding out about?   2 Listen to the poem. Read the words aloud as you listen.

What you will learn in the lesson. There is space for you to show what you think at the end of the lesson. There is also space for your teacher to say what you have learned.

Learning goals		
Our learning goals	I think	My teacher thinks
I can talk about why waste is such a problem.	☺ ☹	☺ ☹ ....

This tells you what the key words are. Key words are in the glossary. The glossary is at the back of the book. You can find out what the key words mean there.

relevant

Activities to help you learn. →

How can we ask relevant questions?

1   Look at Sofia's poster again.
    Amira wants to find out more. She thinks of three questions.
    Draw 🙂 next to the useful questions.
    Draw 🙁 next to a question that is not so useful.

How many children were throwing apples away?

How big are the apples?

Do children eat the apples when the black bits have been cut out?

Interesting facts and information. →

> **Did you know?**
>
> A tally chart is a simple and quick way of counting things. Each thing is shown by a mark, like this |.
>
> If you count five things, you can make a "gate" of five by drawing four marks and the fifth mark is drawn across the middle like this ||||. That makes it easy to count in fives using your five times table.

Useful words.
You can use these words. →

> Why did you show . . . ?   What was the problem with . . . ?
>   Why do you want children to . . . ?

Top tips. Advice to help you do the lesson. →

> **Top tip**
>
> Think about a simple picture that will help people understand about the issue.

🎧 Audio is available on Cambridge GO and in the Teacher's Resource.

🎥 Video is available on Cambridge GO and in the Teacher's Resource.

⤓ Your teacher will have access to free supporting resources through Cambridge GO – the home for all your Cambridge digital content. Visit cambridge.org/go

1 ▶ Where does food come from?

vegetables

crate

Zara

How to cook vegetables

maize

workers

Arun

truck

Sofia

SAMI'S International Foods

Marcus

Dragon fruit, dragon fruit, dragon fruit, mango.

Okra, scallion, leek and potato.

Oranges and passion fruit, spinach and cauliflower.

Apples, ackee, callaloo, karela.

〉 1.1 Where does our food come from?

Learning goals

Our learning goals	I think	My teacher thinks
I can say how I can find out about food.	☺ ☺	☺ ☺ ....
I can show clearly what I have found out.	☺ ☺	☺ ☺ ....

How does food get to us?

01 ▶ You are going to watch a video. Four people are talking about food.

Santha is a farmer.

Rajan is a truck driver.

Abdul has a shop.

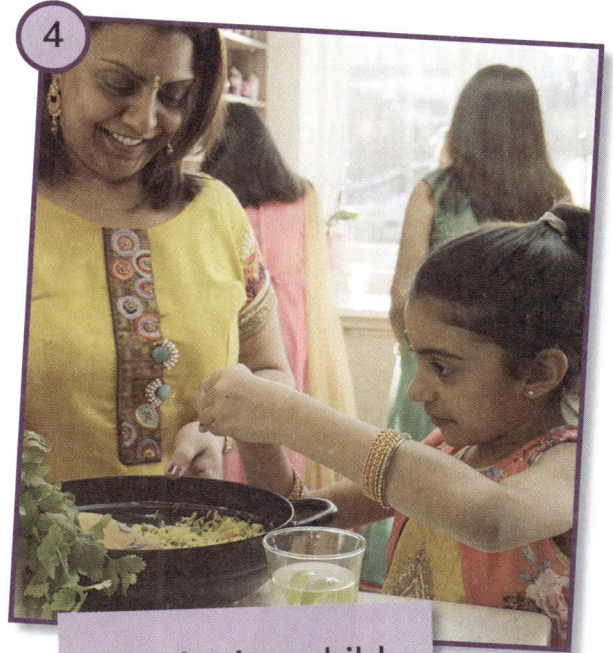

Geetha is a child.

Watch the video and follow the journey that the food takes.

Look at the pictures.

Talk to your partner.

Finish these sentences.

Use these words to help you.

eat   put   packed

sold   grow

First, the cucumbers .... on the farm.

Then, the cucumbers are .... into boxes

and .... onto a truck.

Next, the cucumbers are .... in a shop.

Finally, we can .... the cucumbers.

How can I find out about the food on my plate?

1   Imagine you have a plate of food. How could you find out what happens to your food on its way to your plate?

What do you think you could find out from each of these sources? Look at each of the pictures. Discuss your ideas with your partner.

source
research
label
product
country

By talking to people

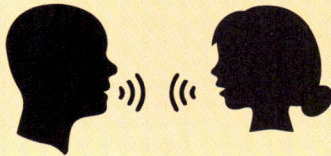

Who could you talk to?

By looking for yourself

What could you look at?

By reading books

What kind of books?

By looking online

What words would you type in?

2   Now work in a group. In your group, discuss these questions. Be ready to share your two best ideas to answer each question with your class.

How can we find out?	
Where does our food come from?	How is our food grown?
How does our food get to our home?	How is the food on our plate cooked?

How can I show information about food clearly?

1 Nerys lives in New Zealand.
She has done some research about the food that she eats.

She looked at the labels on four items of food.

Look at Nerys's food labels.
On each product label, underline the country that the food comes from.

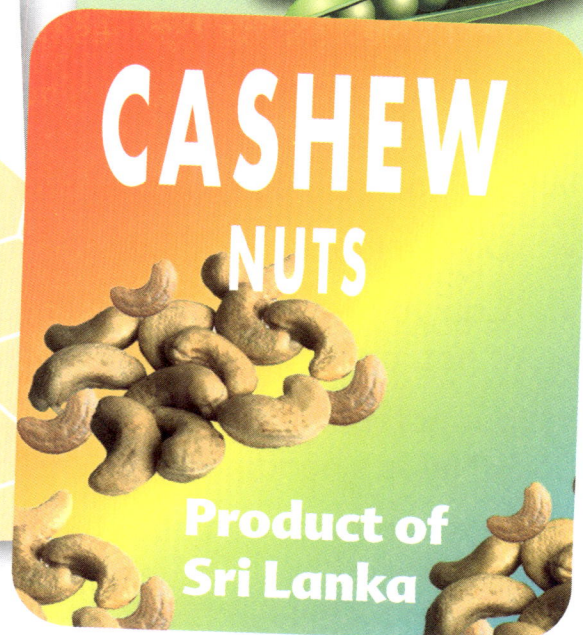

PURE
Butter

PRODUCT OF
NEW ZEALAND

GARDEN
PEAS

GROWN IN NEW ZEALAND

HONEY

Country of origin:
Turkey

CASHEW
NUTS

Product of
Sri Lanka

2   Nerys wanted to find out if the food was made from plants.
She found out by looking up each one online.

She made a table to show all the information she found out.
Look at Nerys's table and answer the questions.

	Comes from New Zealand	Does not come from New Zealand
Is made from plants	Frozen peas	Nuts
Is not made from plants	Butter	Honey

True or false? Circle your answer.

a   Nerys showed information about four items of food.   True   False

b   Nerys found out where her butter comes from.   True   False

c   All of Nerys's food comes from New Zealand.   True   False

d   Some of Nerys's food is made from plants.   True   False

3   With a partner, look at four food labels you have found.

- Do the labels tell you where the food came from?

- Can you tell if the food is made from plants?
  If not, do some more research. Look it up online or in a book.

In your notebook, draw a table like the one that Nerys made.
Copy Nerys's headings but write the name of your country.

Write the information about your food labels in your table.

⟩ 1.2 How far does our food have to travel?

Learning goals

Our learning goals	I think	My teacher thinks
I can find out how far our food has travelled.	☺ ☹	☺ ☹ ....
I can show what I have found out.	☺ ☹	☺ ☹ ....

How can we show where food comes from?

1   Ananya is from Mumbai in India. She found three items of food in her kitchen at home. She has been colouring in a world **map** to show where the three foods come from.

Can you help her to finish her table? You need to find two missing countries and one missing colour.

Look at the countries that Ananya has coloured in different colours.

map

Find those countries on a world map.

Write and colour the information in the table.
The first one has been done for you.

Where does it come from?		Colour on the map
CASHEW NUTS	Cashew nuts from *Sri Lanka.*	
HONEY	Honey from	
White Rice	Rice from	

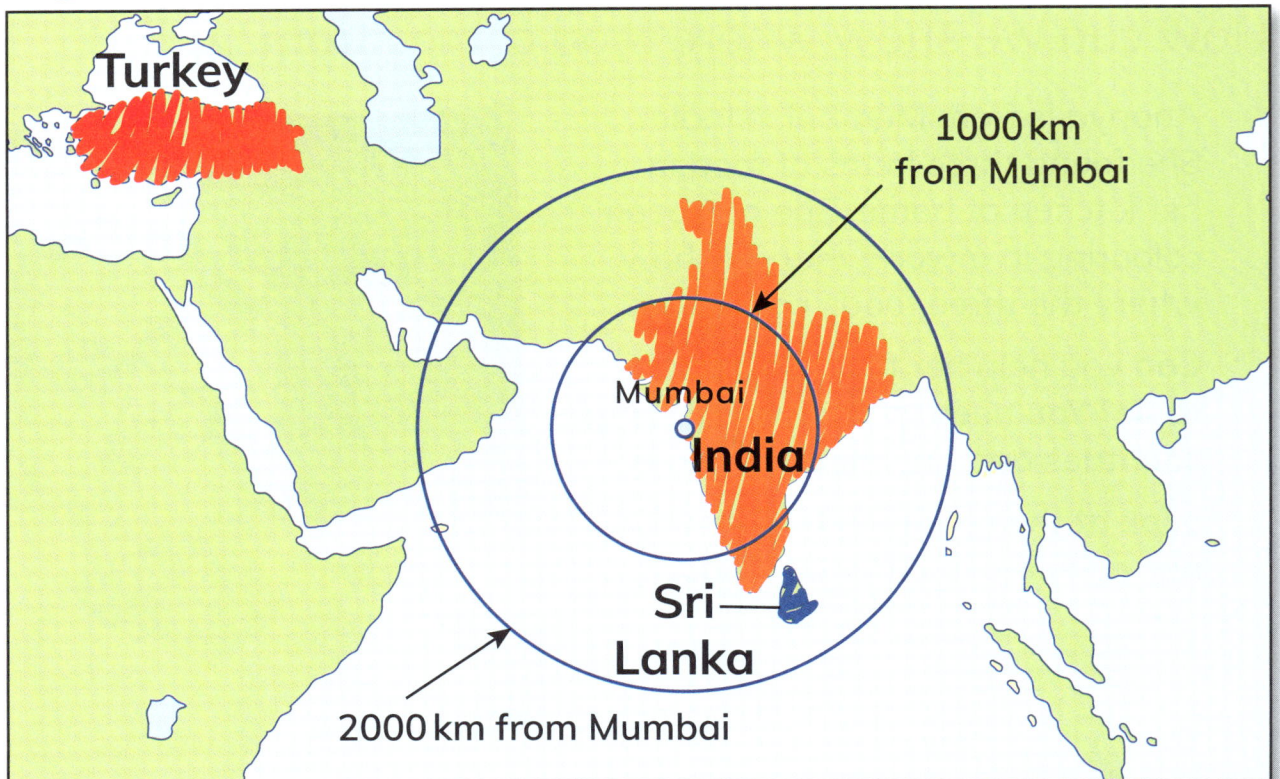

Turkey

1000 km from Mumbai

Mumbai

India

Sri Lanka

2000 km from Mumbai

Top tip

Maps show you different places. You can use them to tell where cities and countries are! Usually, the names of cities are smaller than the names of countries. So you can tell that Mumbai is a city and Sri Lanka is a country by the size of the writing!

2   Ananya drew some circles on her map too. The circles help her to see how far the food travelled to get to her home in Mumbai.

Inside the first circle, the places are near her home. Between the two circles, places are quite far away. Outside the second circle, places are very far away.

Look again at the map on page 18 and write **near**, **quite far from** or **very far from** in each sentence.

Did you know?

A coconut can travel for up to 100 days on the ocean's tide and still grow into a tree!

a   Cashew nuts came from ☐ Ananya's home.

b   Honey came from ☐ Ananya's home.

c   Rice came from ☐ Ananya's home.

3   Finish these sentences by writing the name of the food.

distance

a   .... travelled the shortest **distance**.

b   .... travelled the longest distance.

How far away has our food come from?

1   Now it is your turn to find out how far your food has travelled.
     You will need a map of the world that you can colour in.
     You will need three food labels.

     First, make a chart like the one below.

What is my food called?	Where does this food come from?	This is the colour I have used

2   Work with your group.

     a   Mark the place where you live. Ask an adult to help you draw
          two circles: the first circle will be 1000 km from your home.
          The second circle will be 2000 km from your home.

     b   Colour in your world map to show where your food items
          have come from. Fill in the colours on your chart.

     c   Look at the circles on the map and talk to your group about
          how far each food has come.

     d   Finish these sentences and tick (✓) the correct answers
          to explain where each of your food items has come from.

     .... near   ☐   my home.

                                        quite far from   ☐

                                        very far from   ☐

.... near ☐ my home.

quite far from ☐

very far from ☐

.... near ☐ my home.

quite far from ☐

very far from ☐

> 1.3 What do different people think about where our food comes from?

Learning goals

Our learning goals	I think	My teacher thinks
I can write about what I think.	☺ 😐	☺ 😐 ....
I can say why I think something.	☺ 😐	☺ 😐 ....

Are they for or against the idea?

Sofia, Zara, Marcus and Arun have found out that some food grows on farms near us and some food arrives in ships and planes from very far away.

They have been listening to different people's opinions. Read what they say.

> local   opinion

Some people think it is good to bring in food from far away. They are **for** it.

Some people think it's not good to bring in food from far away. They are **against** it.

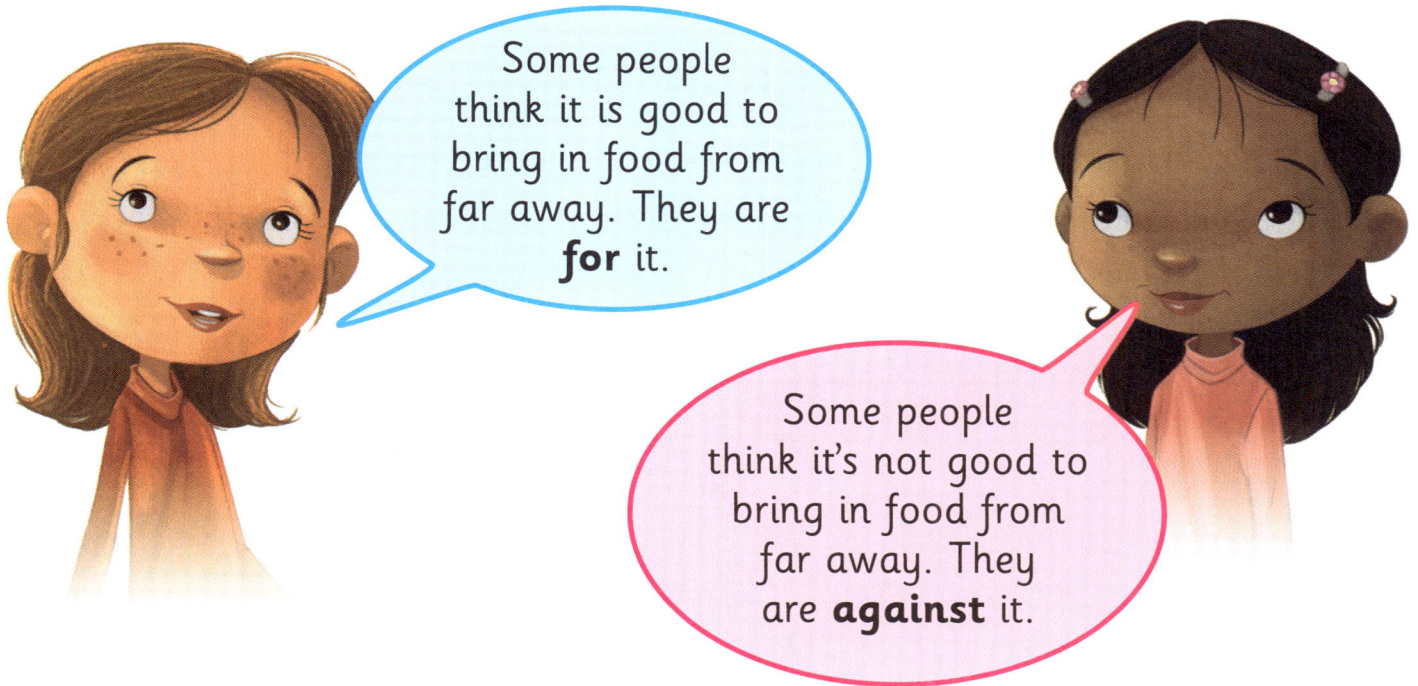

Read the people's opinions. Are they for or against the idea of bringing in food from far away?

Draw ☺ if they are **for**, or ☹ if they are **against**.

a	'I like to buy food that comes from nearby. I know it is fresher.'		d	'If you can buy food from all around the world, you have more choice.'	
b	'It's not good to bring in food from around the world. It makes it hard for local farmers. They need to sell their crops.'		e	'It is not good for the planet. Food from very far away comes by plane. That uses too much fuel.'	
c	'I love eating food from all around the world. I enjoy tasting different meals.'		f	'For me, the cost is important. If food from far away is cheaper, I'll buy it.'	

What should I do when a visitor comes to school?

In Sofia, Arun, Marcus and Zara's class the children are excited.

They are going to talk to two visitors. Both of the visitors work with food. One is a farmer and one is a chef.

Their teacher put this table on the board:

We should ask the	farmer	to tell us	what they like to grow.
			what they like to cook.
			if they sell food to far away places.
	chef		if they buy food that comes from nearby.

Zara has used this table to help her decide what to do when the visitors come to school.

> We should ask the farmer to tell us what they like to grow.

1   Talk to your partner. What else should Zara and Sofia do when the visitors come to their school?

Sofia thought about a question that she would like to ask her visitor.

> Please can you tell us what you like to grow?

2 Talk to your partner. Answer the questions below.

a What other questions should Sofia, Marcus, Zara and Arun ask when the visitors come to their school?

b What should you do when a visitor comes to your school? What questions should you ask when a visitor comes to your school?

Can I say what my opinion is and say why I think that?

With your class, talk to somebody who uses food in their work. For example, perhaps they grow it, cook it or sell it.

a Who did you talk to? ....

b What foods did you talk to you about? ....

c What opinions did they share with you?

....

Now talk to your partner about what the visitor said.

Is your opinion the same as your visitor? Or is it different?

> Our visitor thought ... because ...
> I think ... because ...

Top tips

Listen to your visitor. Ask your visitor questions about what they think. Decide if your ideas are the same or not.

> 1.4 How can we tell other children about the journey of some food?

Learning goals		
Our learning goals	**I think**	**My teacher thinks**
I can help my group make a display about how food gets to our plate.	☺ ☺	☺ ☺ ....

What things will we show in our display?

1   You are going to make a **display** about a meal with your group.
    You will tell people about the **journey** of the **ingredients** in your meal.

🎧 2

Arun and his group are making a display too.
Listen to what they say. Answer these questions with a partner.

  a   Which three foods will Arun and his group find out about?

  b   What do they want to tell people in their display?

2   Talk to your group about your display.
    What meal will you tell people about? Write it here:

    ....

    ....

> display
> journey
> ingredient

Now make a list of the ingredients.

....

....

....

....

....

3   Talk to your group. Tell your group what you already know about these items of food. Listen to what they say.

What happens to our food along its journey?

1   In your group's display, you will need to show pictures to help the other children understand what you tell them. What will you need to show on your display board?

Put a circle around the things that you will need to talk about. You can also draw your own ideas.

						My idea

2   With your group, make a table like the one below.
Leave a lot of space for writing.

Can you answer these questions about the foods for your display?

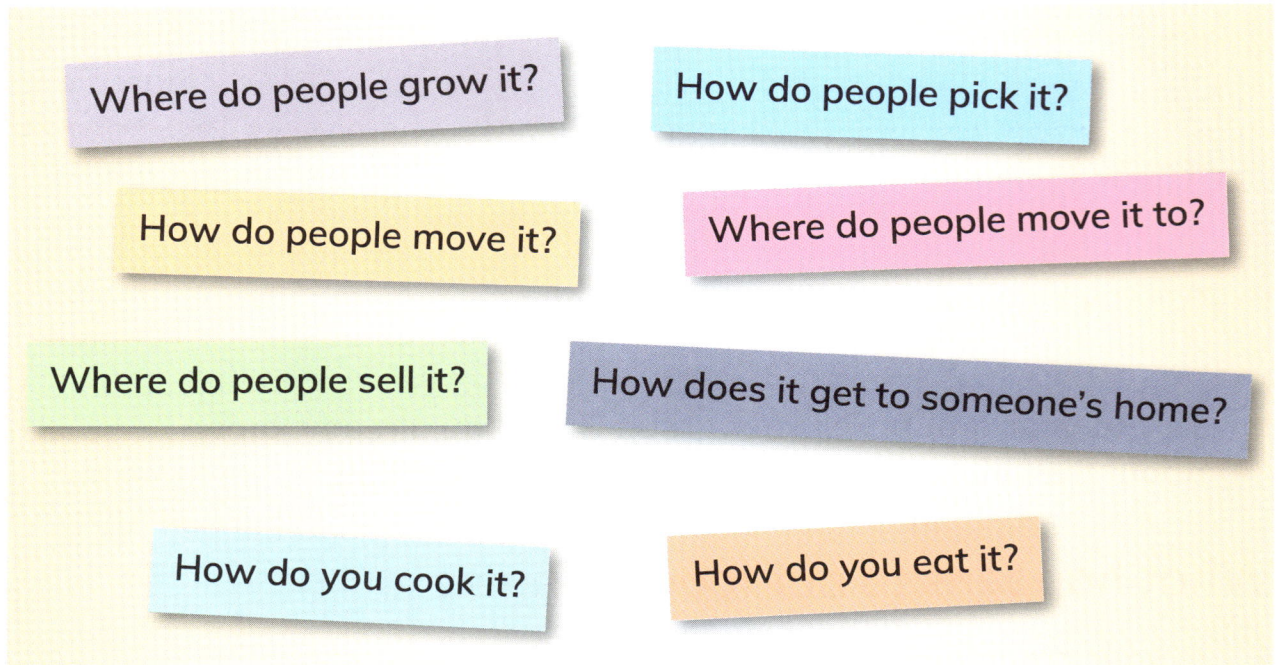

Where do people grow it?

How do people pick it?

How do people move it?

Where do people move it to?

Where do people sell it?

How does it get to someone's home?

How do you cook it?

How do you eat it?

If you know the answer, write it in your table in 'What we know already'.

If you don't know the answer, write the question in the table in 'What we need to find out'.

What we know already	What we need to find out

3   Do some research. Find out the answer to the questions in 'What we need to find out'.

You can ask people or look in books or look online.

> **Did you know?**
>
> Some fruit is picked when it is just ready to eat. If it is not eaten quickly, it will go bad. Some fruit will travel halfway around the world in half a day on an airplane.

How can we work together?

Think about the people who will see your display. How will you help them to understand? What pictures or maps will you need? What will you say? And which person in your group will do what job?

1   Look at the start of Arun's group's plan.

   a   Who is going to say where the ingredients come from?

   b   Who is going to draw a picture of the farmer picking the oats?

Our work plan		
Name	**What we will tell the children**	**What we will show the children**
Sofia	Tell them where the oats, mangoes and bananas come from	A map of where they grow and where we live A picture of a plane carrying them
Arun	Show how the farmer grows the oats Show how the farmer brings in the oats	A picture of oats growing A picture of the farmer bringing in the oats

2   Make a plan for your group. You will need a table like Arun's group used.
    Remember to have a row for every person in your group.

    First, write down what you need to say and what you need to show
    the children. Then write the name of the person who will do each job.
    You can use Arun's group's plan to help you.

Name	What we will tell the children	What we will show the children

3   Write about how you will do your job for the group's display.

    My job for the group's display is ....

    I will tell the other children about   ....

    I will show the other children ....

4   Now prepare your display with your group.

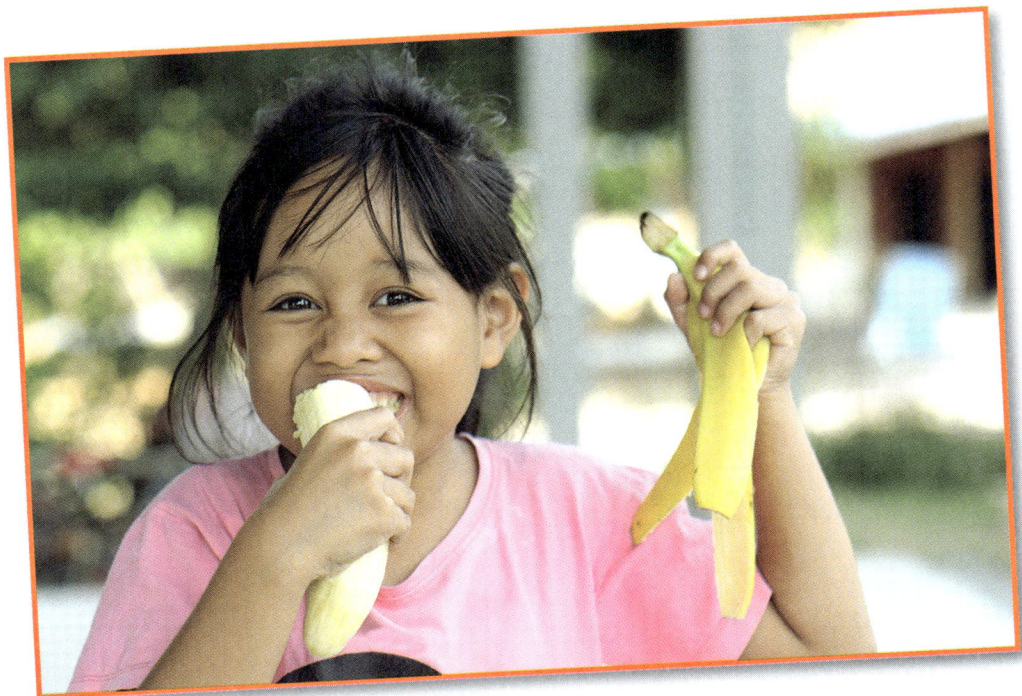

> 1.5 How can we tell other children about how food gets to us?

Our learning goals	I think	My teacher thinks
I can tell other children about our display.	☺ ☹	☺ ☹ ....
I can ask other children about their display.	☺ ☹	☺ ☹ ....
I can answer other children's questions.	☺ ☹	☺ ☹ ....

Learning goals

What shall we say about our display?

Zara and her group are showing their display to other children.
They are telling them about their meal. They are telling them about their meal. They have brought in the vegetables that you need to make the meal.
They are using a big map of the world!

All about mango and banana porridge

🎧 3   **1**   Listen to what Zara and her group are saying.
What is each child showing in the picture? Why?

Talk in your group then finish these sentences:

Arun is showing ....

Marcus is showing ....

Sofia is showing ....

Zara is showing ....

2 Now think about what each person will say in your group's display. Practise with your group. Point to things when you are talking about them.

Checklist

Did you remember to do all these things?

✓ Say what meal you are talking about.

✓ Say what your ingredients are.

✓ Say where they come from.

✓ Say how they get to the place where you live.

✓ Say how they are grown.

✓ Say how you use the ingredients.

What relevant questions can we ask?

1 Zara, Marcus, Arun and Sofia have finished their display. Their friends want to find out more about the things in their display. They have thought of three questions.

relevant

Draw ☺ next to the relevant questions.

Draw ☺ next to a question that is not so relevant.

a Why do the oats travel by ship?

b What do you have for your evening meal?

c Why is there a string by the picture of a mango?

2 With a partner, think of three more relevant questions that other children in Zara's class could ask them. Write them down.

> How does the farmer . . . ?   When do . . . ?
>
> Where does . . . ?   Why . . . ?
>
> How far does . . . ?

....

....

....

What can we find out from other children's displays?

1 Work with other groups who made different displays.
Follow the instructions.

My group's display	The other groups' displays
Talk about your meal	Listen!
↓	↓
Listen to the children's questions. Answer the questions.	Ask a relevant question. Listen to their answer.

2   In your notebook, write about one display that was interesting. Write about:

- the things you saw in the display

- the things the other children said.

> I listened to . . .
>
> They talked about . . .
>
> First, I thought that . . .
>
> Now I know . . .
>
> It was interesting because . . .

> 1.6 What have we learned?

Learning goals		
Our learning goals	**I think**	**My teacher thinks**
I can talk about the ideas I had in this project.	☺ ☺	☺ ☺ ....
I can talk about good ideas that other children had.	☺ ☺	☺ ☺ ....
I can talk about what I learned in this project.	☺ ☺	☺ ☺ ....
I can talk about something that helped me to learn in this project.	☺ ☺	☺ ☺ ....

What do I know? What can I do?

Marcus, Zara, Arun and Sofia have been thinking about
what they have learned in this project.

I now know some vegetables that grow near here.

I now know how to find places on maps.

I now know what a bitter gourd is.

I now know how to tell other children about a display.

Read back over your book, starting at page 10.

Think about:

- the new facts you have learned
- the new skills you have learned.

Talk to your partner. Now explain your ideas.

What do I know?
I have learned about these foods . . .
I now know that . . .
What can I do?
Now I know how to . . .
I learned this because . . .

How did we help each other?

Talk with your group about the things you did together in the project.

What did you do to help your group? Ask your group for their ideas about how you helped them.

Say what other children did to help you.

Tell your group two sentences about how you helped each other in each part of the project.

> I helped my group to . . .
>
> My group helped me to . . .

What helped us to learn?

Sofia learned something in her project.
She also reflected on what helped her to learn. Read what she wrote.

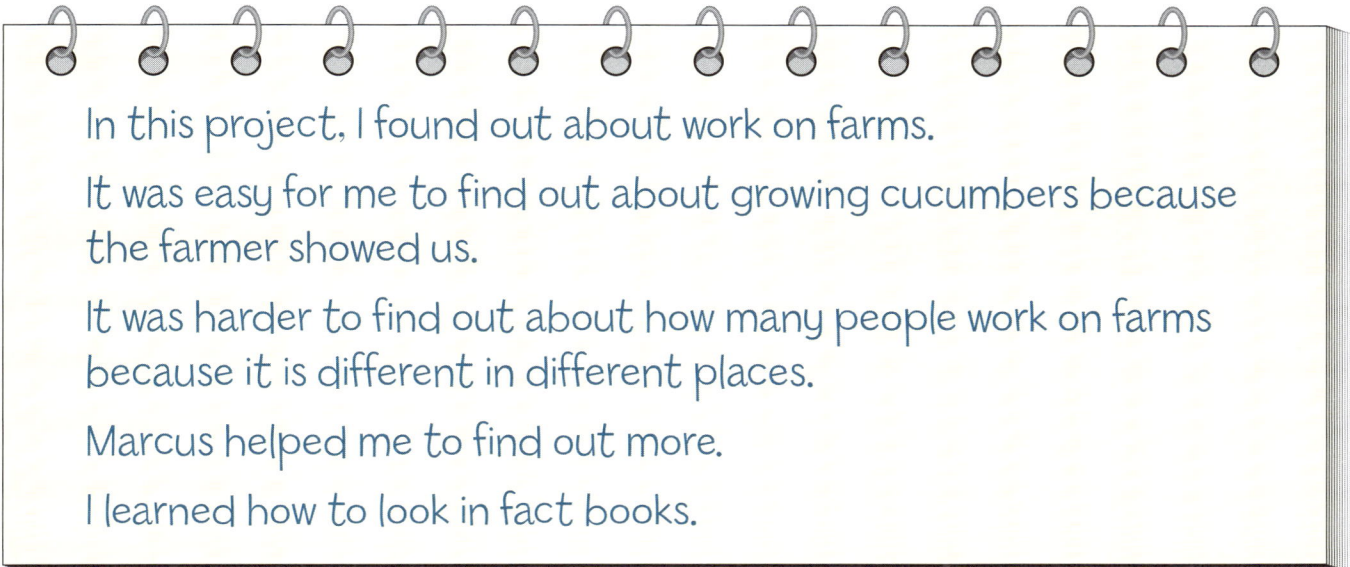

In this project, I found out about work on farms.

It was easy for me to find out about growing cucumbers because the farmer showed us.

It was harder to find out about how many people work on farms because it is different in different places.

Marcus helped me to find out more.

I learned how to look in fact books.

In this this project, I found out about ....

It was easy for me to find out about ....

because ....

....

It was harder to ....

because ....

.... helped me to find out more.

I learned how to ....

....

What happens if we waste things?

Getting started

1 Look at the picture.

- Where are the children?
- What are they doing? Why?
- What different kinds of rubbish can you see?

2 Read and listen to the poem.

Say the words of the poem.

Point to the things that are mentioned in the poem.

Sofia

Arun

litter picker

fishing net

plastic straw

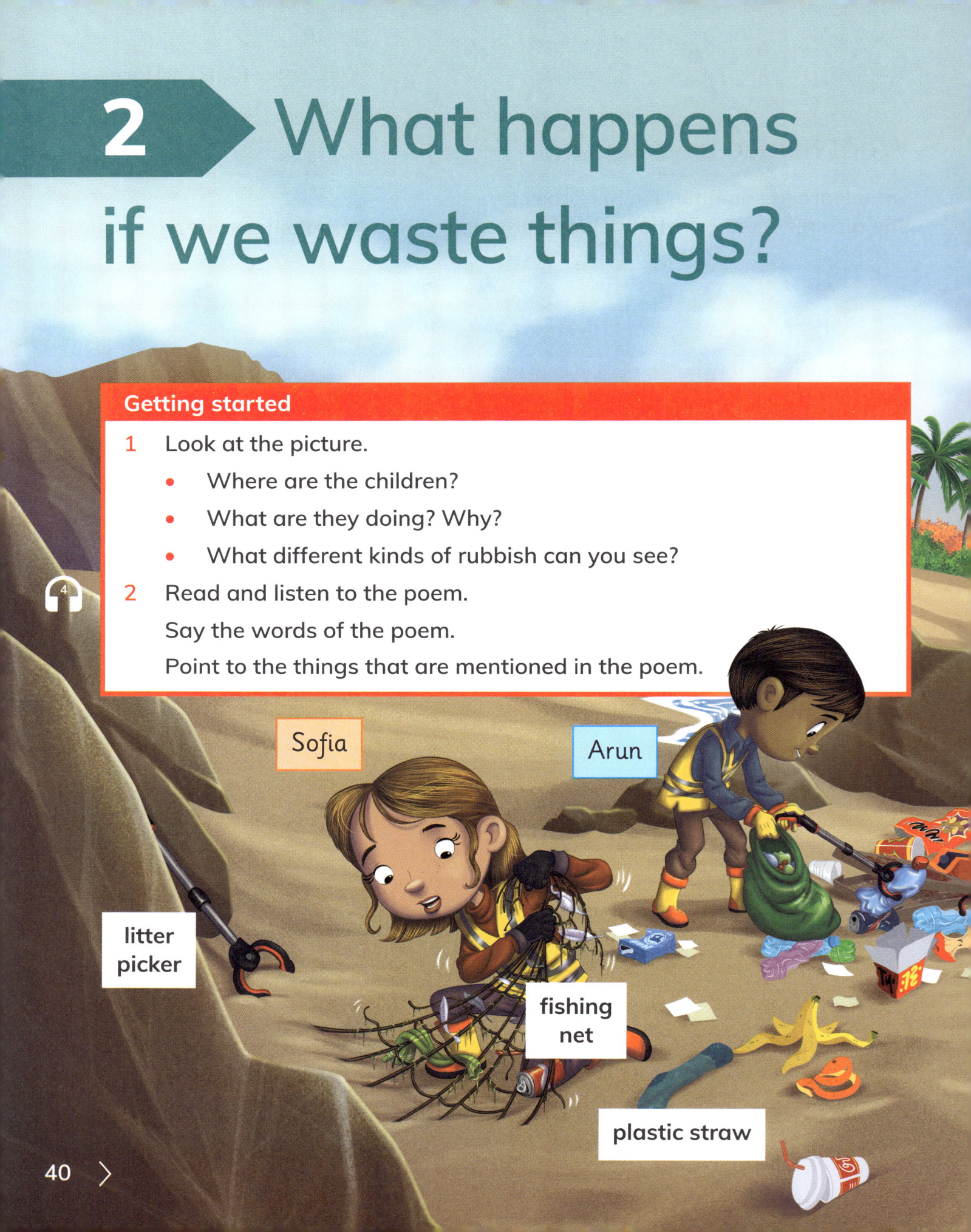

The time has come to clean the beach.
The waste must go. We'll take some each.
We don't want plastic in the sea.
We want it clean for you and me.
Let's put gloves upon our hands.
Clean up the bottles and the old tin cans.
Let's make sure we pick it all up.
Then take away the wrappers
and the plastic cups.

Community Clean-up

Marcus

Zara

cans

food wrapper

bin

❯ 2.1 What is waste and why is it a problem?

Learning goals		
Our learning goals	**I think**	**My teacher thinks**
I can talk about why waste is such a problem.	☺ ☹	☺ ☹ ....

What do people waste?

Every day, people all around the world **throw away** things. Some of the things could be used again.

They also use more water and electricity than they need.

When that happens, it is called **waste**. It is not good to waste things.

> **throw away**
>
> **waste**

1   What are these people wasting? Talk to your partner.

water   electricity   clothes

1

A family are eating dinner together in their kitchen. But there are lights on in every room.

2

Sara wore this costume once for a party when she was little. Now it is too small. She is going to throw it away.

3

Kimiko was washing her parents' car. She has gone away. She has left the water on.

2   Finish these sentences:

In photo 1, the family are wasting ....

In photo 2, Sara will be wasting ....

In photo 3, Kimiko is wasting ....

Why is waste a problem?

1   Marcus wanted to find out more about waste. He talked to people at home and at school. He asked them what waste they had seen.

He wrote what they said but his notes got mixed up. Can you help him match them up?

The first one has been done for you.

consequence

Street cleaner

Supermarket worker

Teacher

School cook

What waste have you seen?

Children do not put lids back on pens after they use them. So the pens dry up and do not work any more.

People drop plastic bottles and bags in the street.

Children take too much food at lunch time and throw it in the bin.

Sometimes people forget to bring their own bags. So they have to buy a lot of new plastic bags.

What is the consequence?

We need to clear them out of the drains so that we don't get floods.

We need to buy and cook more food. It is such a waste to put good food in the bin!

I have to put the pens in the bin and the school has to pay for new pens.

Factories have to make more plastic bags. Plastic is not good for the environment.

2   How could we stop these kinds of waste?
Talk to your partner. Think of three ideas.

What waste have you seen?

1   Talk to your group about
these questions.

- Have you seen somebody
throwing something away?

- Have you seen somebody
using something that
they don't need to?

I have seen
people keep the car
engine on when the car
has stopped. This is a
waste of petrol. It smells
horrible, too.

2   Draw one of the problems
that your group discussed.

3   Describe the problem. Write what the consequence is.

....

....

Sometimes people . . .   This is a problem because . . .

〉 2.2 Where can I find more facts and ideas about waste?

Learning goals		
Our learning goals	**I think**	**My teacher thinks**
I can find a good source of ideas about how to reduce waste.	☺ ☺	☺ ☺ ....

What do we need to find out?

1   Arun and his friends have been learning about waste.

poster

They have decided they want to make a **poster** to make people think about waste.

They have found three ideas so far.
Which two of these ideas are most useful for this project?

Please turn off the lights when you leave the room

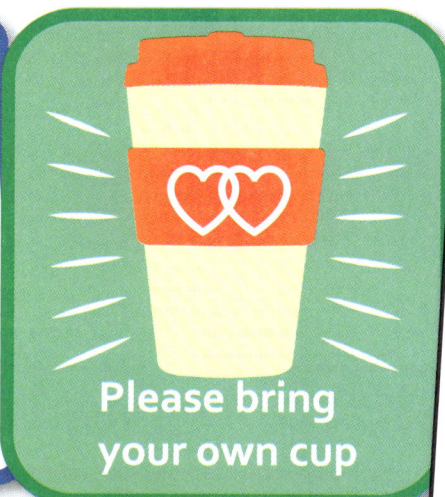

Please bring your own cup

Please walk in the corridor

2   Talk to a partner. Discuss these questions.

   a   Do you do the things in the two useful pictures?

   b   What will happen if more people do these things?

   c   What will happen if nobody does these things?

3   Talk about your answers with your class.

reduce

What is a good source of information?

1   If we want to find out useful ideas, we need to find sources of relevant information.

Sofia wants to find out how to **reduce** the amount of food that children waste.

She has found some sources. Which ones would be the best for her to use?

Look at each source and draw a star or a face in the box.

a very useful source	☆
quite a useful source	☺
not a very useful source	😐

The Anti-Waste Recipe Book

Where your food comes from

How to Cook Fish

Ida Haddock

DON'T TAKE MORE THAN YOU CAN EAT!

2   Explain your answers to your partner.
    Here's an example:

> This is a very useful source because it has ideas to stop people wasting food.

3   Sofia wanted to find out how to reduce the amount of food that children waste and throw away.

    What kind of waste would you like to find out about?

    Talk to your group.

    Finish this sentence.

    We would like to find out how to reduce the

    amount of .... that children ....

waste-saving idea

symbol

recycle

reuse

What can I find out from sources?

Work with your group.

1   Find some sources.

    Make sure they are good sources for finding **waste-saving ideas**.

> **Did you know?**
>
> You can sometimes find this **symbol** on cans, food packages and many other things. It means that you can **recycle** that item. You need to put it in a special bin for recycling. The item will be taken to a factory and used again.

2   Draw and write some waste-saving ideas that you find out
    from your sources.

Think about things you can **reuse**, things you can recycle
and ways to reduce what you use.

Things we can reuse	Things we can recycle	Good ways to reduce what we use

3   Choose one waste-saving idea that you could try for yourself.
    Finish the sentence and draw a picture to show your idea.

A good way for me to reduce waste

would be ....

....

....

....

〉 2.3 How can I find out if people are reducing their waste?

Learning goals

Our learning goals	I think	My teacher thinks
I can find out how people are reducing waste.	☺ ☺	☺ ☺ ....
I can show what I found out in a table.	☺ ☺	☺ ☺ ....

What could we do to reduce waste?

1 Zara and her friends have some ideas for different ways to reduce waste. They have written a note about each idea. Match the correct symbol to each note. The first one has been done for you.

a
Use your own cup when you get water from the tap. Don't leave the tap running.

b
Take a bag with you when your family goes shopping. Don't just get a new bag every time.

c
Put apple cores in a compost box. Don't put them in the rubbish bin.

🎧 5

2   Zara wants to find out how her friends reduce waste.
Listen to Zara talking to them.

   a   What questions does she ask?

   b   Which friend does all the three things that Zara asks about?

   c   What do Zara's other friends say?

3   Talk to a partner.

   Which of Zara's ideas have you and your partner tried?

   Which of these ideas have you and your partner not tried?

How can we find out how many people reduce waste?

1   Zara wanted to ask the same questions about waste to
20 children. She made a chart to record their answers.

   She asked the questions and she did a **tally**.

   Zara wanted to ask the same questions about waste to 20 children.

   Here are Zara's questions:

   Do you use your own cup again and again when you drink from the tap?

   Do you take a bag with you when your family goes to the shop?

   Do you put your apple core on the compost.

tally

> ## Did you know?
>
> A tally chart is a simple and quick way of counting things.
> Each thing is shown by a mark, like this |.
>
> If you count five things, you can make a "gate" of five by
> drawing four marks and the fifth mark is drawn across the
> middle like this ||||. That makes it easy to count in fives using
> your five times table.

Zara's chart looked like this:

Question about saving waste	How many people do it?	Total
Do you use your own cup more again and againwhen you drink from the tap?	₩₩ ₩₩ ₩₩ |||	18
Do you take a bag with you when your family goes to the shop?	₩₩ ₩₩ ₩₩	15
Do you put your apple cores on the compost?	₩₩ |||	

Look at Zara's chart. Answer the questions.

a   Zara forgot to write the number in the last 'Total' box.
    Can you write it for her?

b   Which action to reduce waste was the most popular?

    ....

c   Which action to reduce waste was the least popular?

    ....

What questions can we ask other children in our class?

1   Now you are going to find out what children in your class
    do to reduce waste.

    In your group, choose three waste-saving ideas to ask other
    children about.

> **Do you ever . . . ?**   **Does your family . . . ? Can you sometimes . . . ?**

Write the three questions that you will ask the other children.
You can look at Zara's questions for ideas.

....

....

....

2   Make your chart. Your chart will be like the one that Zara made.
Write or draw your three waste-saving ideas in the chart.

3   Ask your questions to the children in your class.
Record what they tell you by using a tally.

4   Count the total for each idea. Write it in the chart.

Which action to reduce waste is most popular?

Which action to reduce waste is least popular?

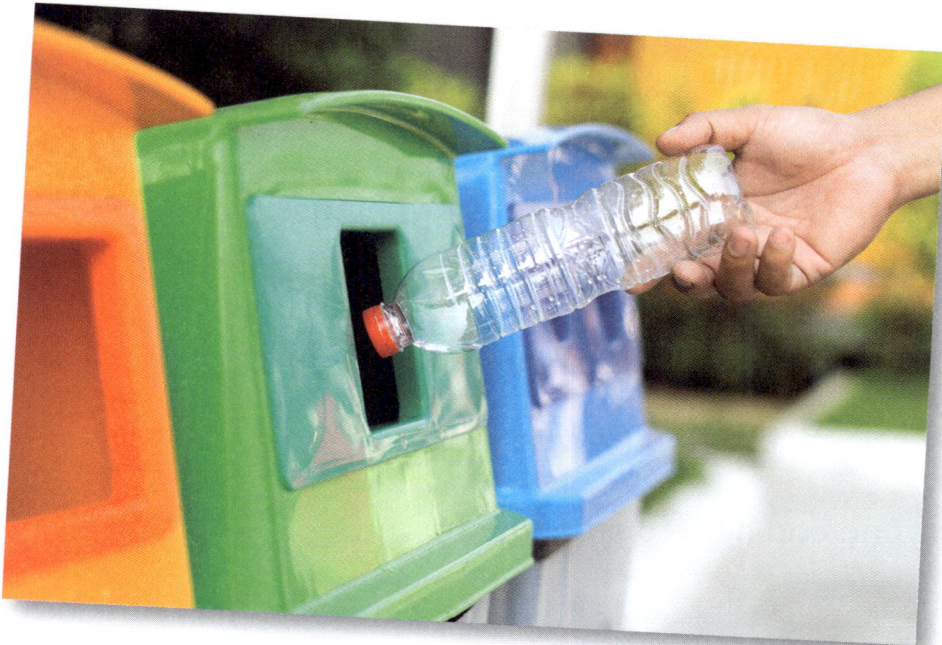

› 2.4 How can we make posters with a message?

Learning goals

Our learning goals	I think	My teacher thinks
		☺ ☹
I can think of ideas to help my group make posters.	☺ ☹	....

What will our message be?

1   You are going to make posters with a group. Your posters will be about waste and what we can do to stop it. All the group's posters should be about the same kind of waste.

message

First, watch the video. Answer the questions with your group.

   a   How can we cut waste by using less?

   b   How can we cut waste by reusing things?

   c   How can we cut waste by recycling things?

2   What do you think is the **message** of the video?

   a   Only scientists know how to stop waste. ☐

   b   Everyone can help to stop waste. ☐

3   In your group, think of some things that children in your school could do to reduce waste. Write down your two best ideas.

....

....

4   What will be the message of your poster?

Our message will be ....

....

How will we show our message?

1   Marcus and Sofia are talking about their group's poster.

> We will make posters for the school canteen because some children take too much food, and then it goes in the bin.

> Our message will be 'Yes to good food. No to bad waste.'

What kind of picture could Marcus and Sofia put on their group's poster? Tell your group.

2   Now it's time to plan your poster. Talk to your group. What do you want people to understand?

Glass

Container

Single-use

Cardboard

Did you know?

If you put food waste in a compost box instead of a bin, it can reduce the rubbish in the bin by 30%.

Rubbish put in bins

Food waste | Other non-food waste

3   What will you write on your poster?

Write some ideas here

You can reduce ....

You can reuse ....

You can recycle ....

4   Talk to your group about pictures for the group's poster.
Draw your ideas.

Our ideas

Top tip

Choose a picture that gives a very clear message. People who look at your poster will need to understand what you would like them to do.

How should we work together?

1   You are going to work with your group to make a plan for your posters.
    First, look at Sofia's group's plan.

Name	Idea for reducing food waste
Sofia	Can I have a bit less, please?
Arun	Put food you haven't opened on a special table not in the bin. Someone else can eat it.
Marcus	Stay and finish your food. You can chat to your friends.
Zara	Cut out little black bits on your fruit. The rest is yummy!

What do you think about Sofia's group's ideas?
Could they work in your school? Talk to a partner.

2   Now make a plan with your group. Make one row for each person.
    Decide what you will put on your group's poster.

Name	Idea for ....

3   Make your poster with your group.

〉 2.5 How can we talk about our posters?

Learning goals

Our learning goals	I think	My teacher thinks
I can tell other children about our posters.	☺ 😐	☺ 😐 ....
I can ask other children questions about their posters.	☺ 😐	☺ 😐 ....

How can we tell other children about our poster?

🎧 6 **1** Sofia's teacher has arranged for Sofia to speak to a child from a different school. The child's name is Amira. Sofia is going to tell Amira about the poster she has made.

Look at Sofia's poster.
Then listen to what they say.

Tick (✓) the things that Sofia
and Amira talk about.

Wasting food

Compost

Plastic waste

Healthy food

Don't throw me away!

Ask an adult to cut out
the black bit. The rest of
me is very tasty!

2   Listen again. Answer these questions.

a   Why did Sofia make a poster
about apples?

b   Why does Amira think the poster
is good?

Talk about your answers with a partner.

3   Now look at your poster.
What will you tell other
children about your poster?

Talk about your ideas with
your group.

Top tips

- Talk about the
message of
your poster.

- Say what people
were wasting.

- Say what you want
children to do to
stop the waste.

How can we ask relevant questions?

1   Look at Sofia's poster again.

Amira wants to find out more. She thinks of three questions.

Draw 😊 next to the useful questions.

Draw 😕 next to a question that is not so useful.

How many children were throwing apples away?

How big are the apples?

Do children eat the apples when the black bits have been cut out?

2   Think of two more relevant questions for Amira to ask Sofia about her poster.

> **Why did you show . . . ?**   **What was the problem with . . . ?**
>
> **Why do you want children to . . . ?**

Talk about your ideas with a partner. Write your best questions.

....

....

....

What can we find out from other children's posters?

1   Work with another group who made posters with a different message. Follow the instructions.

My group's poster	The other group's poster
Talk about it!	Listen!
↓	↓
Answer questions.	Ask questions.

2   Which of the other group's posters had the clearest message?
Write about it here.

The clearest message I saw was ....

....

I chose this message because ....

....

> 2.6 What have we learned?

Our learning goals	I think	My teacher thinks
I can talk about the ideas I had in this project.	☺ ☺	☺ ☺
I can talk about good ideas that other children had.	☺ ☺	☺ ☺
I can talk about what I learned in this project.	☺ ☺	☺ ☺

Learning goals

Sofia has been thinking about what she has learned in this project.

Waste is a problem because food goes in the bin. Farmers work hard to grow good food for us to eat. I can help to reduce waste by not throwing away apples with spots. I can cut the spots out.

What do I know? What can I do?

What have you found out in this project?

Talk to your partner. Below are some questions to help you.

What do I know?
Why do you think waste is a problem?   How can you help to reduce waste?

What can I do?
What ways do you know to reduce waste?   How did you learn this?

How did we help each other?

Talk with your group about the things you did together in the project.

What did you do to help your group? Ask your group for their ideas about how you helped them.

Say what other children did to help you.

With your group, talk about:

- When you were doing research.
- When you were thinking of ideas for your posters.
- When you were making your posters.
- When you were talking to other children about your posters.

> I helped my group to . . .   My group helped me to . . .

What helped us to learn?

Marcus has been thinking about what he has learned with his group in this project.

He also reflected on what helped him to learn. Read what he wrote.

In this this project, we found out about food waste.

It was easy for us to find out about what went in the bin. We looked.

It was harder to find out about how to do a good poster. Lots of posters were for grown-ups.

To find out more we asked Amira what worked in her school.

We showed the children in our school how to not waste apples on our poster.

Write about what you learned in this project.

In this project, we found out about ....

....

....

It was easy for us to find out about ....

....

....

It was harder for us to find out about ....

....

....

We showed the children in our school ....

....

....

3 ▶ How can we be active and healthy?

Getting started

1   Look at the picture. Answer the questions.

   a   Where are the children?

   b   What is each child doing?

   c   Have you tried any of the activities in the picture?

   d   What games do you like playing?

2   Listen to the poem. Read the words aloud as you listen.

Zara

exercise bike

leaflets

Try out a new activity!

Marcus

Arun

coach

trampoline

Sofia

running track

stalls

cricket bat

It's great to go out and do exercise.
Try it yourself and you'll soon realise
Why sport is fun, it is for everyone.
You can bike, bat a ball or go for a run!

〉 3.1 How do we feel when we are active?

Learning goals

Our learning goals	I think	My teacher thinks
I can talk about what other people do when they are active.	☺ ☺	☺ ☺ ....
I can talk about activities that I could try out.	☺ ☺	☺ ☺ ....

What helps us to stay healthy?

1 Look at the photos. Answer the questions with your group.

   a   What are the children doing? How do these things help us to stay **healthy**?

> healthy

   b   What happens to you if you *don't* do these things?

   c   Think of three other things you can do to keep healthy.

2 Watch the video. What kind of physical activity did you see in the video?

> physical activity
>
> active

3 Watch the video again.
Circle the correct answer.

a Our bodies change when we do something active.   True   False

b Our feelings change when we do something active.   True   False

c We always have to do physical activity in a special place.   True   False

How can we do healthy things all through the day?

Zara and Arun are making a timetable of a healthy day.

What else could they put in their timetable?

Draw or write your ideas in the timetable.

Morning	Lunchtime	Afternoon	Evening	Night time
eat a healthy breakfast	....	....	....	sleep well ....

Did you know?

Do you run a lot and can you keep going? This is called endurance.

Can you swing across the bars on a climbing frame, using your arms? This is called strength.

Can you bend and touch your toes? This is called flexibility.

How does it feel when we are active?

1   Sofia and Marcus have been writing in their diaries.
    Read what they wrote.

Sofia's diary

Wednesday 23rd April

I was so active yesterday. It was 'Walk to School Wednesday', and we did swimming at school too. I was excited because I floated like a starfish all by myself! We played tag at break-time all together. It was fun. Fozia couldn't catch me – hurray! In the evening, I was tired.

Marcus's diary

We had a special sports afternoon and all the parents came to watch. We had a relay race. I was a bit disappointed because we didn't win, but I was proud of myself for trying really hard. All of us in my team were very happy.

Underline the words that show you how Sofia and Marcus felt during their active day.

2   Think about the most active day you have had.
    Think about what you did. Think about how you felt.

    In your notebook, write about your active day, like Sofia and Marcus did – or you could draw some pictures.

    Talk to your partner about what you did and how you felt.

What activities could we try out for ourselves?

Zara and Arun have been watching people do physical activities in their **area**. They are talking about the ones that they would like to try out.

area

> I have seen children learning tai chi. I would like to try it. It looks fun.

> I want to ride up the hill in the park in less than one minute.

Talk to your group about different ways to be active in your area. Make a list together.

Tell the others in your group which ones you would like to try.

I would like to try . . .   I want to . . .

〉 3.2 How can I find out about places to do physical activity?

Learning goals

Our learning goals	I think	My teacher thinks
I can find out facts about places to do physical activity near me.	☺ ☹	☺ ☹ ....
I can find out what other children like to do for physical activity near me.	☺ ☹	☺ ☹ ....

What can we find out from maps?

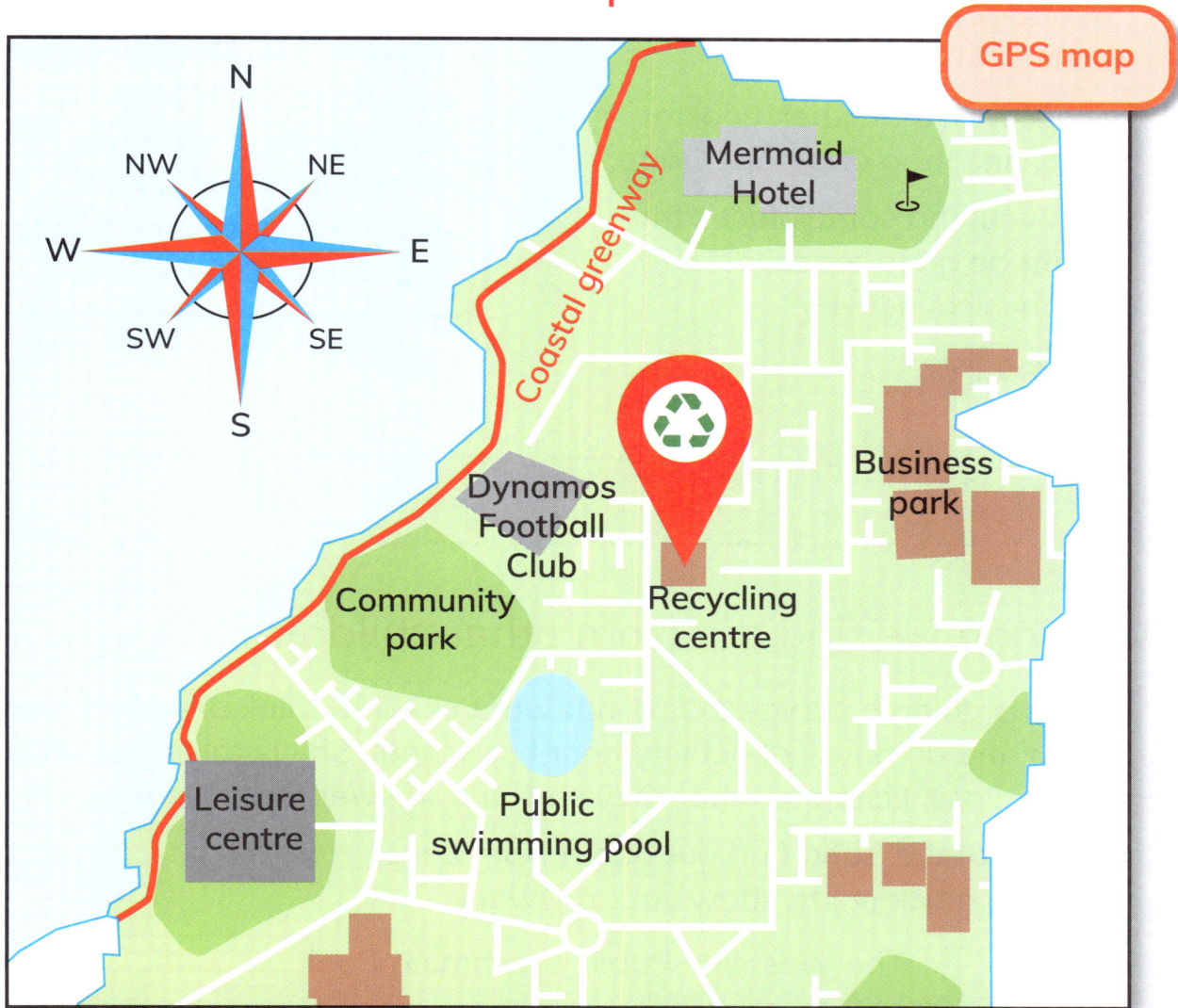

GPS map

N
NW   NE
W   E
SW   SE
S

Coastal greenway

Mermaid Hotel

Dynamos Football Club

Community park

Recycling centre

Business park

Leisure centre

Public swimming pool

1   Sofia wanted to find out where she could go to do physical activity in her area. She looked for information online using a computer in her class. She found a **GPS map** of her town.

Look at Sofia's map. Can you find some places that might be good for children to do physical activity?

Circle them.

Top tip

Look at the writing on the map and the shapes on the map too. Look for big open spaces with no buildings – these might be good places for children to do physical activity.

2   Now you are going to find out about good places for physical activity in your area.

Work with a partner. Look at an online map or a paper map.

Can you find some places that might be good for children to do physical activity?

Make a list.

| **Did you know?** |
| There is a worldwide project called the 'Daily Mile'. Four million children in 90 countries run a mile every day at school. A mile is around 1600 metres. |

....

....

What can we find out from other children?

1   Sofia is doing a survey to find out what children think are good places to go and do physical activity near her school. She is talking to children in her class. Listen to what they say, and answer the questions.

a   What did Sofia find out about from Zara?
Use a tick (✓) to show your answers.

☐   The Westside Public Swimming Pool

☐   The Dynamos Football Club

☐   The community playground opposite her school

b   What fact did Sofia find out? ....

....

c   What opinion did Sofia find out? ....

....

2   Sofia finished asking her questions to the rest of her class.

She showed her final results like this:

Place	Have you been there?	What can you do there?
Westside Public Swimming Pool	5	Swimming lessons
Dynamo Football Club	1	Football coaching
Community playground	16	Run and chase

Talk to your partner and decide if these sentences are true or false:

The first one has been done for you.

Fewer than ten children have been to the Westside Swimming Pool.   (True) / False

Ten children have been to the Dynamo football club.   True / False

More than ten children have been to the community playground.   True / False

You can do swimming lessons at the Westside Public Swimming Pool.   True / False

How can I find out what the children in my class think?

Work with a partner. Make a table like the one that Sofia made.

Choose three places to do physical activity in your local area.
Write the names of the places in your table.

Follow the instructions.

How to do a survey

1   Decide on what questions you will ask.
     Write the questions in the table.

2   Now ask your questions to the children in your class.

3   Record children's answers using a tally.

4   When you have finished asking your questions,
     add up the tally and show what you found
     out clearly.

Have you ever been to . . . ?

What was your opinion of . . . ?

Top tip

It is a good idea to think about how you will show your information before you ask questions.

> 3.3 How can I find out more about activities I can do?

Learning goals		
Our learning goals	**I think**	**My teacher thinks**
I can find information about something I would like to try out.	☺ ☹	☺ ☹ ....
I can give my opinions about something I would like to try out.	☺ ☹	☺ ☹ ....

What would be a good source of information for me?

At the sports try-out day, Zara really liked trying her hardest on the exercise bicycle.

What she really wants to know is where she can go to get better at cycling. Zara looked at different sources of information and found facts about cycling.

Zara did some research.

1   With your group, make a list of different activities that children can do in your area. Decide on an activity that you would like to find out more about.

How could you find out more information about the activity?

- by talking to people

- from books

- online.

> **Did you know?**
>
> Many activities don't need special equipment. If you try out lots of different activities, you can find out which ones you like best.

The activity we have chosen is ....

How will you find out more about this activity? Talk about your ideas in your group.

How can experts help?

1   An **expert** is going to talk to you. Your teacher will tell you who they are. This person knows a lot of information about physical activities that you might like to try.

expert

We will be talking to ....

We can find out information about ....

2   With your partner, think of some relevant questions that you could ask your visitor.

Do I need to wear special clothes?

Make a list.

....

....

....

Top tip

Try to find out where you can go to do this activity and if you need to bring anything with you!

Where can . . .   What do you . . .   Why is this . . .

3   Listen carefully to your visitor. Ask your questions.

Top tip

You can write down key words while your visitor is speaking to help you remember!

What activities would you like to try?

Zara talked about the activity she would like to try. She wrote her opinion.

What activity would you most like to try? Talk to your partner.

An activity I would like to try is cycling. A place where I could do it is Westside cycling academy.

I would still like to know about different bikes. It would also be good to know what clothes are best.

An activity I would like to try is ....

A place where I could do it is ....

What would you like to still find out about?

I would still like to know about ....

It would also be good to know if ....

⟩ 3.4 How can we make a stall together?

Learning goals		
Our learning goals	**I think**	**My teacher thinks**
I can find out and talk about a healthy activity in our area.	☺ ☹	☺ ☹ ....
I can help my group to make a leaflet.	☺ ☹	☺ ☹ ....

What will my group's stall be about?

You are going to set up a **stall** with your group. People will come to visit your stall.

You will give them a **leaflet** with information about an activity or a place to do an activity.

If your leaflet is about an activity, you can also show them how to do this activity.

> stall
>
> leaflet

1   First, choose what kind of information you will give.

Option 1

All about a physical activity children can do in your area.

Our idea

Option 2

All about a place near you where children can do different physical activities.

Our idea

Make your decision as a group. (Circle) Option 1 or Option 2 and then write what your stall will tell people about.

                    Option 1   Option 2

Our stall will tell people all about ....

2   What messages will you give in your leaflet?
    With your group, tick (✓) the ones you choose.

Our activity is fun. ☐   Our activity is for everyone. ☐

Our activity makes you healthy. ☐   Our activity is for people who like a challenge. ☐

Our activity is easy to do in our area. ☐   Our activity will help you to make new friends. ☐

How should we plan our leaflet together?

1   Zara's group chose option 2. They worked together to plan their leaflet. Look at Zara's group's leaflet to get some ideas for your leaflet.

First, they used a checklist. Read the notes that they wrote.
Do you like the children's suggestions? Why or why not?

> **Checklist for your leaflet**
>
> - **Write about the activity you can do.**
>   Ride your bike in the District 5 park.
>
> - **Write about where you can do the activity.**
>   There is a bike track in District 5 bike park.
>
> - **Write about why you should do it.**
>   fun   friends   skills
>
> - **Show pictures.**
>   You need to see the bike park.

2   Next, they made their leaflet.

Here it is.

> # Fun on a bike!
>
> **Have you ridden your bike in District 5 bike park?**
>
> **The bike track is fun to do with friends.**
>
> **You can learn new skills.**
>
>
>
> ## It is so much fun!

In your groups, answer these questions about Zara's group's plan. Be ready to share your ideas with the class.

a   What place are they writing about?

b   What activity is the leaflet giving information about?

3   Now make a plan with your group like Zara did with her group. Decide on your message.

What do you want children to try out?

4   Create your leaflet with your group.

Have you ever … ?

It is great fun to . . .

. . . is a good place to . . .

. . . is fun to do with friends.

You can learn . . .

What else will we have on our stall?

When visitors come to your stall, you can give them your leaflet. You also need to decide what to say to your visitors and what to show them.

Zara is talking about the things they will show on their group's stall.

We will have a photo of the cycling track. We'll also have a cycling helmet. We can show people how to wear it safely.

- Are there any objects, pictures or clothes that you could show to people who visit your stall?

- Can you show them a skill they will need when they do your activity?

Talk to your group. Draw or write about what you decide.

What we will show on our stall

> 3.5 How can we talk to children about activities to do in our area?

Learning goals		
Our learning goals	**I think**	**My teacher thinks**
I can talk to other children about good activities to do in our area.	☺ ☐	☺ ☐
I can ask other children questions about good activities to do in our area.	☺ ☐	☺ ☐
I can answer other children's questions.	☺ ☐	☺ ☐

How can we persuade children to take part in an activity?

1   Look at the picture of Marcus's and Sofia's stall. Marcus's group are telling Zara why she should try a game called gulli danda.

Listen to what they say. Tick (✓) the things they talk about.

Where you can play gulli danda.   ☐

Why gulli danda is good for you.   ☐

How to win the game.   ☐

The skills you need.   ☐

2   Listen again. Answer these questions.

   a   What questions does Zara ask?

   b   How do Marcus and Sofia answer Zara's questions?

   c   How do Marcus and Sofia try to **persuade** Zara to try this activity?

persuade

3   Now think about your stall. What will you tell the children who visit your stall? Talk with your group. Practise what you will say.

What questions will we ask at other children's stalls?

1   Look at Marcus and Sofia's group's stall again.

Zara wants to find out more information because she wants to try out gulli danda now.

She thinks of three questions to ask Zara and her group.

Draw ☺ next to the most useful question.

Draw ☺ next to a question that is quite useful

Draw ☹ next to the least useful question.

Can you use a normal stick to play gulli danda?

Who is the best gulli danda player in the world?

What are the rules for gulli danda?

2   With a partner, think of two more relevant questions for Zara to ask.

....

....

What can we find out from other children's stalls?

1 Work with other groups who made different stalls.
   Follow the instructions.

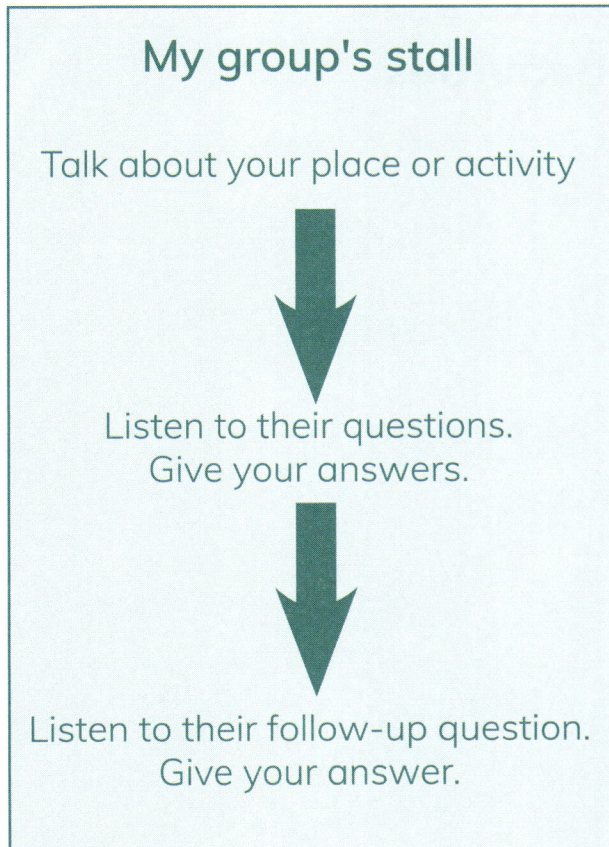

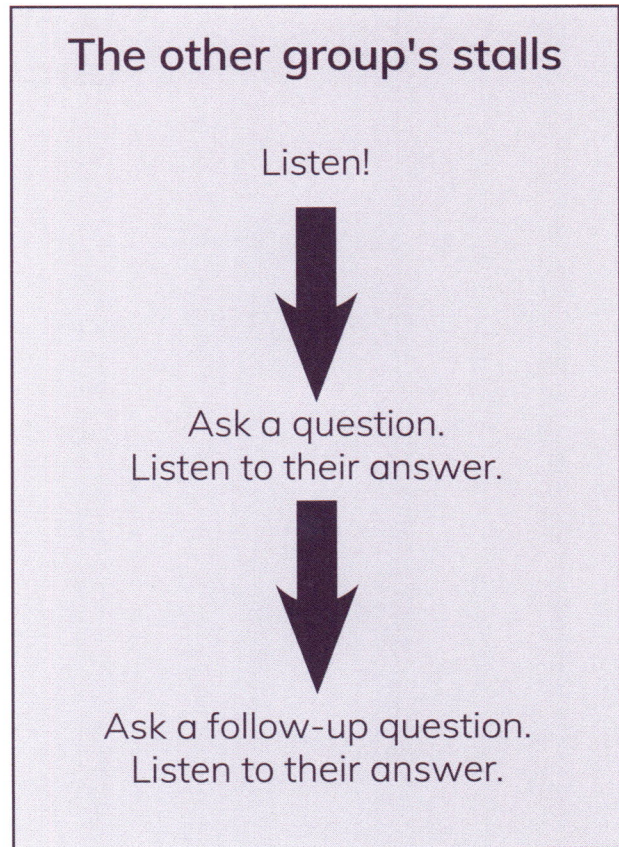

My group's stall	The other group's stalls
Talk about your place or activity	Listen!
↓	↓
Listen to their questions. Give your answers.	Ask a question. Listen to their answer.
↓	↓
Listen to their follow-up question. Give your answer.	Ask a follow-up question. Listen to their answer.

Top tip

A follow-up question is a second question that you ask after the first question when you want to get more information. For example:

- Is there a football club near our school?
- Yes, there's Dynamos football club.
- Can children our age join the club?

The question 'Can children our age join the club?' is the follow-up question.

2   What was your favourite stall?

Draw it here and write about it below.

**My favourite stall
about activities**

My favourite stall was ....

I liked it because ....

....

> 3.6 What have we learned?

Learning goals

Our learning goals	I think	My teacher thinks
I can talk about the ideas I had in this project.	☺ ☺	☺ ☺ ....
I can talk about good ideas that other children had.	☺ ☺	☺ ☺ ....
I can talk about what I learned in this project.	☺ ☺	☺ ☺ ....
I can talk about something that helped me to learn in this project.	☺ ☺	☺ ☺ ....

What do I know? What can I do?

What have you found out in this project?

Explain your ideas in each box.

What do I know?
It is good to do exercise because . . .   .   A good place for me to do exercise is . . .   .
What can I do?
Now I know how to . . .   .   I learned this because . . .   .

How did we help each other?

Talk with your group about the things you did together in the project.

Ask them to say what they think you did to help your group.

Say what other children did to help you.

I helped my group write some good sentences for our leaflet.
I had not played Gulli Danda before. Sofia and Marcus
showed me lots of times so I watched and copied them. – Zara.

Read what Zara wrote. Then write two sentences about how
you helped each other.

....

....

What helped us to learn?

Sofia wrote what she learned to do in this project.
Then she wrote what helped her to learn.

I have learned how to find out more about places.
Something that helped me was a map of our area.
The map had a key.
I learned that a map can help you know what a place is like even
if you have not been there.

Write one thing you have learned how to do.

I have learned how to ....

Write one thing that helped you to learn.

Something that helped me was ....

....

4 ▶ What is it like to move here?

Let's welcome a new family
To their new home
They need some information
On their mobile phone.
What will help them find out
The things they need to know,
All about the area
And where they'd like to go?

HOSPITAL

PARK

OOL

BANK

AIRPORT

Marcus

> 4.1 What does it mean to move to a new place?

Learning goals		
Our learning goals	**I think**	**My teacher thinks**
I can talk to other children about what it is like to move to a new place.	☺ ☺	☺ ☺ ....
I can say what I have found out about an issue by using numbers.	☺ ☺	☺ ☺ ....

How can we find out what a new area is like?

Marcus saw the new family arriving in his town.
He wondered why they had come.
He found some information on a website.

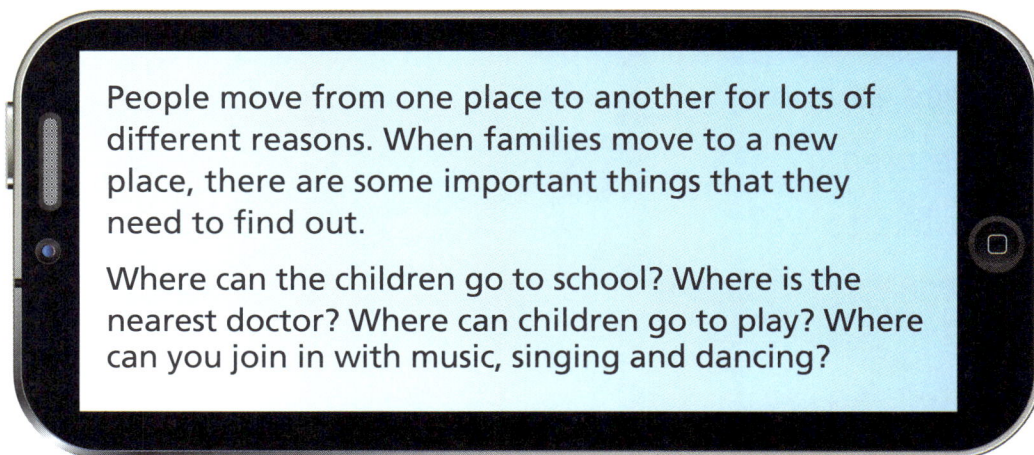

People move from one place to another for lots of different reasons. When families move to a new place, there are some important things that they need to find out.

Where can the children go to school? Where is the nearest doctor? Where can children go to play? Where can you join in with music, singing and dancing?

1   Marcus wanted to find out more about the important things children need to know when they move. He talked to his Uncle Kwame, who moved a long way from his first home when he was at school.

Listen to their conversation.
Answer the questions.

(Circle) **True** or **False**.

a	Marcus had to move to a new area.	**True**	**False**
b	Marcus's uncle had to move to a new area.	**True**	**False**
c	Everything about moving to a new place is easy.	**True**	**False**
d	Marcus's uncle had all of the important things he needed in his new area.	**True**	**False**

2   Look at these pictures. They are things that families who move to a new area can find out about. Listen to the audio again. With a partner, circle the ones that Marcus and Uncle Kwame talk about.

Finding a doctor

Finding work for parents to do

Making music

Finding a new school

Finding places to play

What can we learn about people who move to new places?

Arun has been finding out District 5 and the people who live there.

design
infographic
issue

He has been looking at infographics.

An **infographic** is a way of showing facts. It uses pictures as well as words and numbers.

Information shown in this way can help us to understand **issues**.

1 Look at these three infographics.

Almost one person out of every three people in the District 5 is a child.	One out of every ten people who have moved to District 5 is a child.	Since the year 2000, the number of people who have moved to District 5 has grown by almost half.

With a partner, finish the sentences.

a Almost one person in every .... people in District 5 is a child.

b One out of every .... people who move to District 5 is a child.

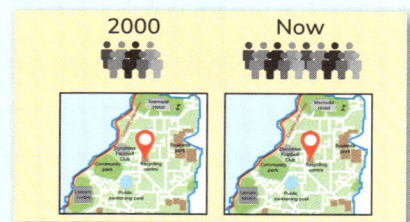

c Since the year 2000, the number of people who have moved to

District 5 has ....

by ....

What can I choose to do in my school?

Marcus, Zara, Arun and Sofia have been talking about the things that they enjoy doing in school.

They have been talking about the things that they can choose to do. They have been thinking about the things that help them understand how everything works.

1   When you move to a new school, you need to know about all the different ways to find help.

Read Sofia's **example**. Then think of two more examples that are true for you and your group.

example

If I need to find out what day we have swimming, I can look on the class timetable.

I can ask my ....

I can look at the ....

2   When you move to a new school you need to know about all the different things you can choose to do.

Read Arun's example. Then think of two more ideas with your group.

I enjoy choosing a library book and talking about it. I like to share my ideas.

I enjoy choosing ....

I like to ....

› 4.2 What do we need when we start at a new school?

Learning goals		
Our learning goals	**I think**	**My teacher thinks**
I can find out other children's ideas about our school.	☺ ☺	☺ ☺ ....
I can show what I have found out about other children's ideas.	☺ ☺	☺ ☺ ....

How can we show new children what they need to know about their new school?

Arun, Marcus, Zara and Sofia want to help new children understand the things they need to know about their new school.

They have found out that they know lots of things about their school. They have decided to tell new children about four of them.

1   Look at these pictures.
    Then read the parts of the sentence that go with them.

    Can you help Arun, Marcus, Zara and Sofia finish these sentences?

We always talk to an adult

if we are feeling ....

....

....

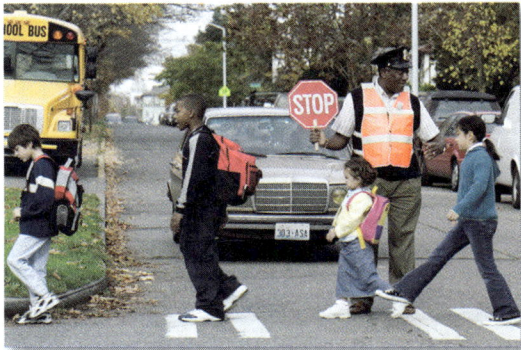

If we cross the road,

we always ....

....

....

When it is dinner time,

we always ....

....

....

When it is music time,

we always ....

....

....

2   Think about what happens in your school. Draw a picture to show a new child something they would need to know.

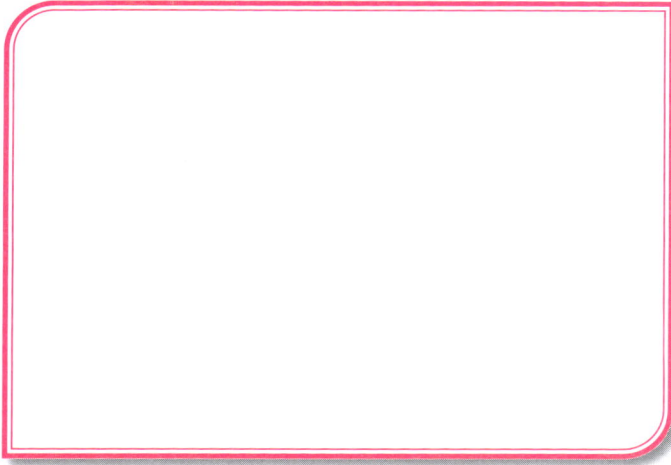

Top tips

Think about:

- things that help keep children happy, healthy and safe in your school
- things that help children feel like they **belong**.

belong

3   Write about what you have shown in your picture.

happy   healthy   safe

In my picture I have shown how you can ....

....

This helps you to ....

How can we tell new children what they need to know in their new school?

Marcus, Zara, Arun and Sofia are going to tell what they need to know in their new school about how to stay healthy, happy and safe.

They want to tell new children what they need to know to feel like they belong.

Often, things that keep us happy, healthy, safe and help us feel like we belong are linked to the things we should do.

Good food keeps us healthy.

So we should not waste good food.

1   They have learned that things that keep us happy, healthy and safe, and help children feel like they belong are linked to the things we should do. Draw a line between them. One has been done for you.

1 We feel happy when people are kind to us.

a So we should tell an adult if we notice something that is not right.

2 We feel safe because the adults in our school look after us.

b So we should try our best.

3 We feel proud when we do well.

c So we should be kind to other people.

4 We feel like we belong when we are included in activities

d So we should help other children to feel welcome and to join in.

2   What helps you to stay happy, healthy and safe?
    Talk to your partner and complete the sentences below.

.... helps me to feel happy because ....

....

.... helps me to be healthy because ....

....

.... helps me to stay safe because ....

....

.... helps me feel like I belong because ....

....

How can we find out other children's opinions?

Marcus was thinking about the new children in his school.
He did some research to find out how children stay happy, healthy,
safe, and feel they belong.

Marcus also found out different ways that he and his friends can help
new children in their class. He asked some questions and he made
notes about the replies.

How do you help other children stay safe in school?

How do you try your best in school?

I remind children about where it is not safe to run.

I always use the learning goals to help me check my work.

Work with other children in your class. Take turns to ask questions. Find out some ways that the children in your class stay happy, healthy and safe in school.

Talk to the children in your group about what the other children say.

Ask the children in your class:

- What makes you happy in school?
- What helps you to stay healthy?
- What helps you to stay safe in school?

How can we write what we have found out?

1   Marcus wrote a report about his research. He wanted to explain how things work in his school for a new child.

Marcus wanted to tell a new child how we help each other feel happy, healthy and safe.

Read what he wrote.

My report – by Marcus

Children in my class are happy when they play together.

Children in my class eat fruit for their snack to help them stay healthy.

Children in my class stay safe when they walk inside – they do not run.

Finish these sentences about Marcus's report.

a   The children in Marcus's class are happy when

....

b   The children in Marcus's class ....

.... to help keep them healthy.

c   The children in Marcus's school stay safe when ....

....

2   Now write about the children in your school.

a   The children in my class are happy when ....

....

b   The children in my class ....

.... to help them keep healthy.

c   The children in my class stay safe when ....

....

Top tip

Think about how you help other children.

Think about how other children help you.

> 4.3 What would it feel like to move to a different place?

Learning goals		
Our learning goals	**I think**	**My teacher thinks**
I can say what I think it would be like to move somewhere new.	☺ ☺	☺ ☺ ....

What can we find out from a person's story?

1 You are going to watch a video about people moving to new countries.

Read these questions, then watch the video. After you have watched, discuss your answers with your partner.

a How is Jassie travelling to his new home?

b Who is travelling with him?

c How did Jassie's dad travel to their new home?

d What different ways can people use to travel from one country to another?

e What reasons do people have for moving from one country to another?

2   Have you ever moved to a new home in a new area?
Can you imagine what it would be like?

Jassie is a child whose family have moved to a new country called Erlandia. He is writing a letter to his cousin.

Hi Ishy,

Mum and Dad are so happy because they love their new jobs here in Erlandia. It has been three months since we moved. There are so many new buildings. Our flat is new. Everything is new here. The food here is different from food back at home. I have tried some new food. Some things are very nice! I am learning how to speak Erlandian.
I can say 'My name is ...', 'Please' and 'Thank you'. I have not started school yet because the school is not finished. They need to put in the electricity and turn on the water. It is hard to make new friends with no school. Some children play outside my flat but they are all bigger than me so I got a bit scared. I would like to play table tennis like I used to, but we have not found a place to play yet.

I miss you and all my friends. Please write soon.

Lots of love,
Your cousin Jassie

How do you think Jassie feels about moving to a new home?
Happy, sad or somewhere in between?

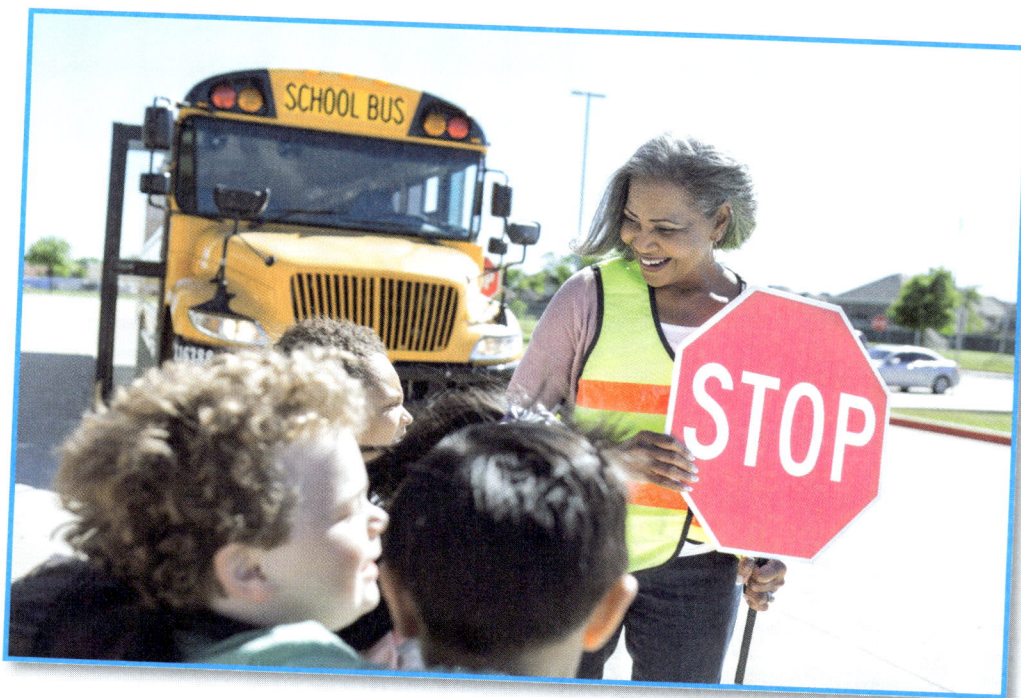

What advice would we give to a new child?

Imagine that you could write a reply to Jassie, or to a different child who has just moved to a new country.

1   What would you say in your letter? What **advice** would you give? Talk about your ideas with your group.

Think about:

*   How he or she would be feeling.
*   What words he or she might like to read.

advice

2   Write your **letter** by placing the right words into the spaces.

strange   three   meet lots of new children

talking to your parents   Erlandia   new

join in with some games   smile   listen carefully

try out the words you know

Dear Jassie,

I know you have moved to .... only ....

months ago. Sometimes it can feel a bit .... when

we move to a new place. Don't worry. This is because so many

things are .... A good way to make new friends is to

.... A good way to

learn a new language is to ....

and .... When your new school

is ready, you will be able to ....

If you are feeling like everything is a bit strange, you could try

....

How could we help children who are new to our school?

Children who are new to the school need to find out about a lot
of new things! When children feel happy, healthy and safe, they are
ready to learn and to join in.

Help them by answering the questions.
Work in your group and write your group's answers in the table.

> **You could try asking . . .**   **It's a good idea to . . .**
>
> **It is important to . . .**   **Why don't you . . .**

What new children need to know	How children can find out in our school
How can I get food and water? How can I be healthy?	....
How can I learn well? How can I relax and play?	....
Who can I talk to if I have a question? Who will listen if I have an opinion?	....
What should I do if I feel upset or unsafe?	....

› 4.4 How can we tell new children what they need to know about our school?

Learning goals		
Our learning goals	**I think**	**My teacher thinks**
I can think of useful information to help children who are new to our area.	☺ ☺	☺ 😐 ....
I can help my group to prepare a role play.	☺ ☺	☺ 😐 ....

What information does a new child in our school need?

Sometimes when we learn, it helps to pretend to be other people. We call this kind of learning **role play**.

role play

You are going to do a role play about a child who is new to your school. You are going to show how other children can help them to feel happy, healthy and safe.

You will need to plan what to say in your role play. Work with your group. Decide what you will say. Decide who will say it.

Arun, Zara, Sofia and Marcus needed some ideas for their role play, so they made a **mind map**. A mind map helps you think of ideas and organise them.

mind map

bring a bottle
and refill it

Public
swimming pool

Water

Health

What do you need
to be healthy?

What do you need
to do well?

Food

Borrow books
from library

School
council

Welcome to
our school!

School
canteen

What do you need
to be happy?

What do you need
to feel safe?

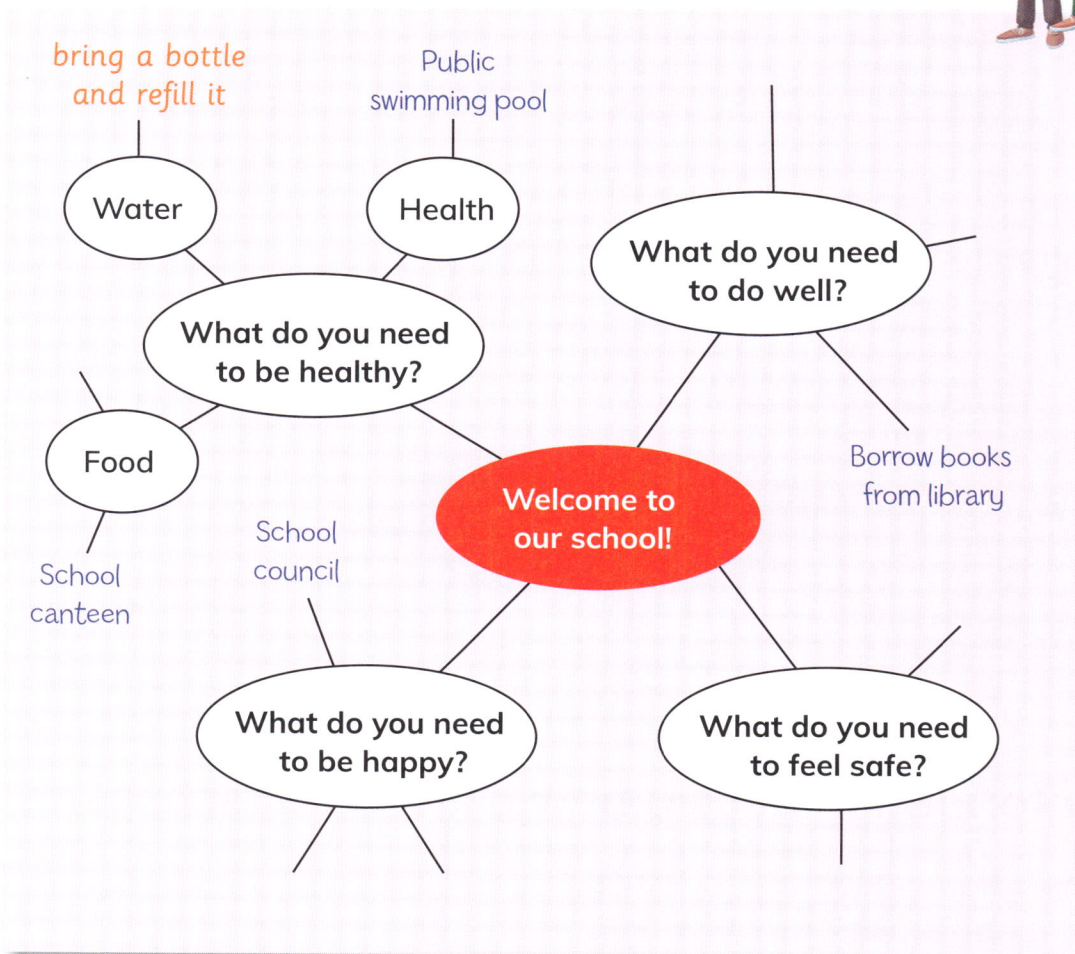

Work with your teacher to make a mind map similar to the one Arun, Zara, Sofia and Marcus made. Think of lots of information that a new child would need to know about your school.

Top tip

Remember what your role play is about. You want to show how a new child will be happy, healthy, feel safe and feel they belong in your school.

What will we say in our role play?

1   Now you have lots of ideas for things to tell a new child in your role play. You need to plan what you will say. Work with your group. Decide what you will say. Decide who will say it.

Our plan for our role play	
What will we say?	Name
1 Welcome the new child	....
2 Say what the role play is for	....
3 Tell them information about:	....
4	....
5	....
6	....
7	....

2   Now practise with your group.

How should we work together?

1   You are going to practise your role play.

First, read Sofia's idea for working together when you are performing.

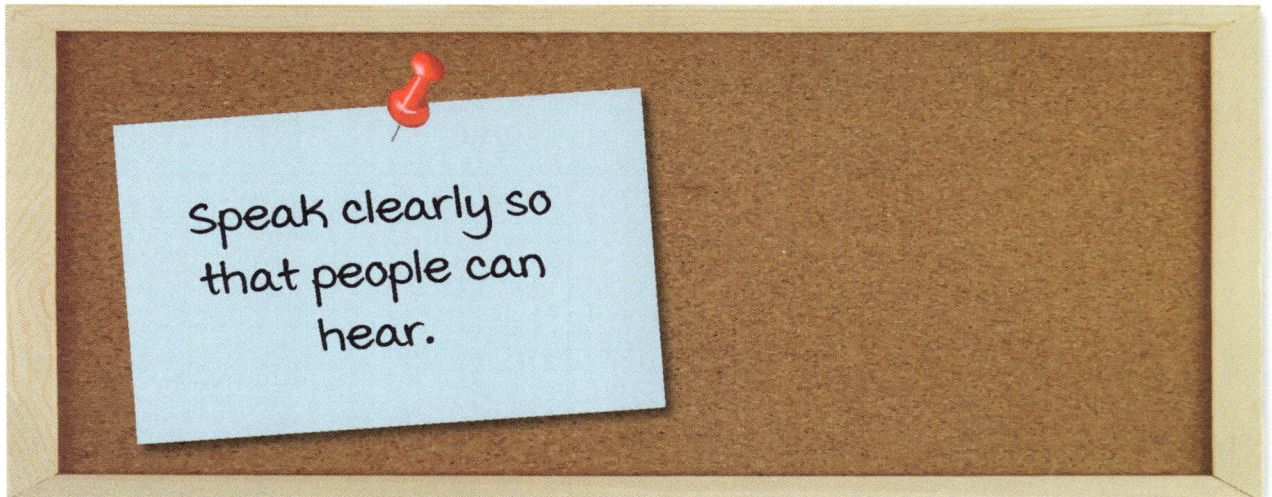

Speak clearly so that people can hear.

With your group, think of some more rules for working together to make a good role play. Write the best two rules here.

2   Now practise your role play with your group.

❯ 4.5 How can we answer questions about our role play?

Learning goals		
Our learning goals	I think	My teacher thinks
I can tell other children about our school.	☺ ☺	☺ ☺ ....
I can ask other children questions about their role plays.	☺ ☺	☺ ☺ ....
I can answer other children's questions about our role play.	☺ ☺	☺ ☺ ....

How can we improve our role play?

Sofia's group have recorded their role play.
They are going to listen to the first part.

improve

1 Listen. Tick (✓) the things you hear the group talk about.

What a new child needs to know. ☐

Good places to play. ☐

What to do in the canteen. ☐

How to **improve** their role play. ☐

2 Read these questions, then listen to Sofia's group again. Answer the questions.

a What useful tips do the children give in their role play?

b What do they want to improve in their role play?

Talk about your answers with a partner.

3 Now think about your role play. How could you improve it? Talk about your ideas with your group.

I like the way . . .   I think we should . . .

Top tips

- Did you give some helpful tips for a new child?
- Did you explain how a new child can enjoy their new school?
- Did you speak very clearly so your words were easy to understand?
- Did everyone in your group have a turn to speak?

4 Perform your role play again. Try to improve it.

What can we find out from other children's role plays?

Work with other groups who performed their role plays.
Follow the instructions.

My group's role play	The other group's role play
Perform your role play.	Watch and listen!
↓	↓
Listen to children's questions. Answer their questions.	Ask a relevant question. Listen to their answer.
↓	↓
Listen to their follow-up question. Give a relevant answer.	Ask a follow-up question. Listen to their answer.

What were the best ideas that we heard?

Marcus has listened to a role play from another class.

Read what he wrote about it.

> I really liked the way that they sang a song to help everyone remember all about their new school.
>
> It was interesting to hear about the Reading with Parents club.
>
> That is good idea for new children because they can read with parents and school staff.

Write about the good ideas that you heard in the role plays in your class.

a   I really liked the way that they ....

    ....

b   It was interesting to hear about ....

    ....

c   That is a good idea for new children because ....

    ....

> 4.6 What have we learned?

Learning goals

Our learning goals	I think	My teacher thinks
I can talk about the ideas I had in this project.	☺ 😐	☺ 😐 ....
I can talk about good ideas that other children had.	☺ 😐	☺ 😐 ....
I can talk about what I learned in this project.	☺ 😐	☺ 😐 ....
I can talk about something that helped me to learn in this project.	☺ 😐	☺ 😐 ....

What helped us to learn?

1   Arun thought about what helped him to learn
in this project. Read what he wrote.

> Listening to Marcus's uncle helped me to learn. I learned about all of the things that change when you move and the things that stay the same. Doing the role play helped me learn too. I had to think about talking very clearly.

Here are some activities in this project that help children to learn. Tick (✓) the things that you liked doing best.

Looking at infographics. ☐   Making a mind map. ☐

Finding out children's ideas. ☐   Showing a role play to ☐
                                              other children.

2   Write about how all of those things helped you to learn.

I looked at infographics. This helped me to ....
....

I found out about other children's ideas. This helped me to
....

I made a mind map. This helped me to ....
....

We showed our role play to other children. This helped me to
....

How have we been good learners?

Sofia, Marcus, Arun and Zara have been thinking about how they have been good learners in this project.

Read what they wrote about each other:

Marcus thinks about other children's ideas carefully. He told us all about another good role play – by Sofia

Zara thinks of new ideas. She came up with loads for our role play mind map. - by Arun

Arun kept working to get the role play finished. He never gives up easily. – by Zara

You can trust Sofia to remember all the things we need. –– by Marcus

Talk with your group. How have you been good learners?

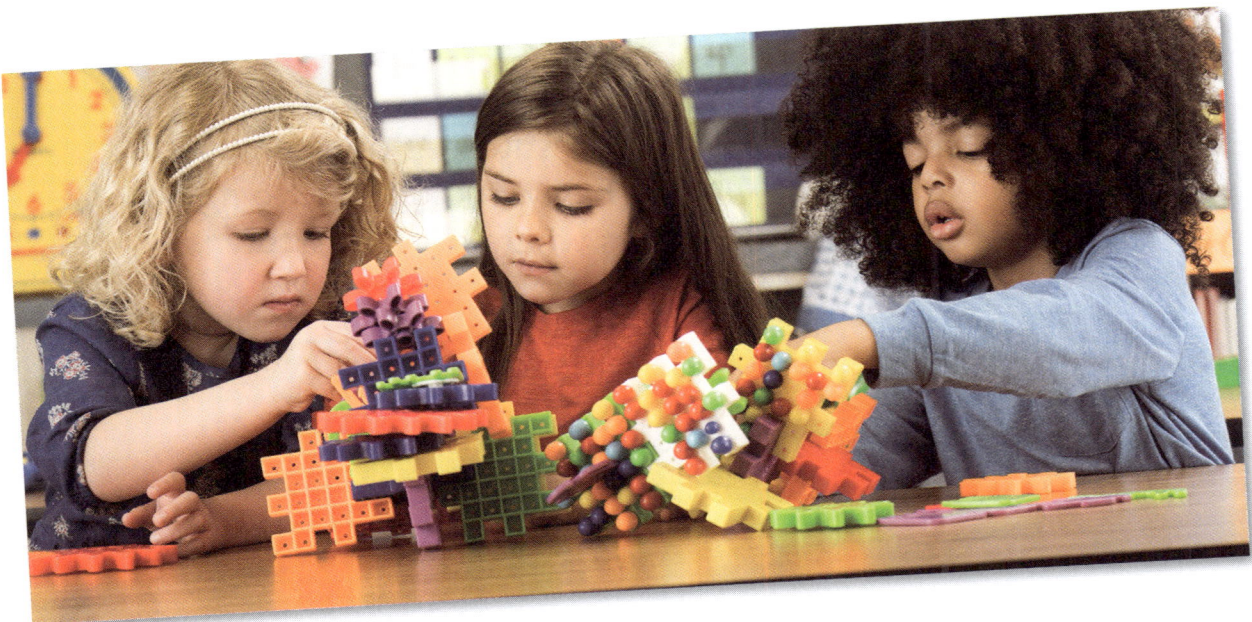

Glossary

active	doing things where you move around a lot
advice	giving ideas about what you think someone should do or how they should do it
area	a place inside of a country or city
belong	feeling like you fit in, or you are a member of a group
consequence	something that happens because of something else
country	a place that makes its own laws and has its own flag
design	to draw or plan something
display	a collection of information, things or pictures for people to look at
distance	how long the space is between two places or things
example	something that shows you what you are talking about
expert	someone who is very good at something or knows a lot about something
GPS map	a map that is made by satellites and computers around the world. They work together to make a picture that shows where countries, towns, roads, rivers, and so on are
healthy	to be strong and well
improve	to get better or to make something better

infographic	a picture or diagram that makes information easier to understand, a way of showing facts
ingredient	a simple food that other, more complicated foods are made from
issue	a subject or problem that people are thinking or talking about
journey	to travel from one place to another
label	a small piece of paper that tells you about the thing it is stuck to
leaflet	a piece of folded paper or a small book that tells you about a topic
local	about or in an area near you, or near the area you are talking about
map	a picture of an area that shows where countries, towns, roads, rivers, and so on are
message	a piece of written or spoken information that one person gives to another
mind map	a way of showing ideas, with lines and circles, with the main idea in the middle and other ideas around it
opinion	a thought or belief about something or someone
persuade	to make someone do or believe something by giving them a good reason to do it
physical activity	movement that you do to make your body strong and healthy
poster	a large piece of paper with pictures and writing that tells people about a topic
product	something that is made or grown to be sold

recycle	to turn things that are old and used up into something new
reduce	to use less or to make something smaller
relevant	information or an opinion that is useful to what is being talked about
research	the study of a subject so that you can discover new facts
reuse	to use again, to find a new use for something so that it does not have to be thrown away
role play	when you role play, you pretend to be another person
source	where something comes from
stall	a table where people give out information or sell things
symbol	a drawing, shape or object that is used to represent something
tally	a way of keeping count of something that happens lots of times, or things you have seen
throw away	to get rid of something
waste	anything that is not wanted that is thrown away or what is left after you have used something
waste-saving idea	a plan to reduce the number of things that you throw away

Acknowledgements

The authors and publishers acknowledge the following sources of copyright material and are grateful for the permissions granted. While every effort has been made, it has not always been possible to identify the sources of all the material used, or to trace all copyright holders. If any omissions are brought to our notice, we will be happy to include the appropriate acknowledgements on reprinting.

Thanks to the following for permission to reproduce images and video:

Unit 1 CR Shelare/GI; sefa ozel/GI; Ariel Skelley/GI; caiafilm/GI; Javier Zayas Photography/GI; Catherine McQueen/GI; Mayur Kakade/GI; Creativ Studio Heinemann/GI; Yamada Taro/GI; bubaone/GI; rambo182/GI; lushik/GI; bounward/GI; vreemous/GI; undefined undefined/GI; Indeed/GI; **Unit 1 video** BBC Universal/GI, CR Shelare/GI, Nikocam/GI, sefa ozel/GI, Ariel Skelley/GI, caiafilm/GI; **Unit 2** Ivan Hunter/GI; LightFieldStudios/GI; EasyBuy4u/GI; PeopleImages/GI; Drazen_/GI; Andreas Selter/GI; XiXinXing/GI; Cunaplus_M.Faba/GI; Sukanya sitthikongsak/GI; oonal/GI; Ariel Skelly/GI; **Unit 2 video** Elyse Lewin/GI, Seabird/GI, thaiview/GI, JK1991/GI, SolStock/GI, FG Trade/GI, SolStock/GI, Pigeon Productions Inc./GI, Many Hands Productions/GI, Imgorthand/GI, SolStock/GI, SolStock/GI, Jim Arbogast/GI; **Unit 3** Tang Ming Tung/GI; FatCamera/GI; Tetra Images/Gi; Asia Images/GI; Robert Niedring/GI; FatCamera/GI; HRAUN/GI; fundamental rights/GI; Artranq/GI; Fran Polito/GI; Halfpoint Images/GI; FatCamera/GI; monkeybusinessimages/GI; aire images/GI; **Unit 3 video** Klaus Vedfelt/GI, Thomas Barwick/GI, BBC Universal/GI, ugurhan/GI, pixdeluxe/GI, recep-bg/GI, kasipat/GI, recep-bg/GI, Nick David/GI, Lighthouse Films/GI, vgajic/GI, pixelfusion3d/GI, staticnak1983/GI, Yamato1987/GI, staticnak1983/GI, South_agency/GI, recep-bg/GI, Yamato1987/GI, Brudder Productions/GI; **Unit 4** FatCamera/GI; Luis Alvarez/GI; Cultura RM Exclusive/Phil Fisk/GI; 10'000 Hours/GI; Mayur Kakade/GI; Catherine Falls Commercial/GI; Andersen Ross Photography Inc/GI; SolStock/GI; Jose Luis Pelaez Inc/GI; FatCamera/GI; FG Trade/Gl; staticnak1983/GI; Jupiterimages/GI; BRIAN MITCHELL/GI; Compassionate Eye Foundation/Robert Daly/OJO Images/GI; Ariel Skelley/GI

Key: GI = Getty Images

Cover by Omar Aranda (Beehive Illustration)